History in the making: York citizens parade over Lendal Bridge and up Station Rise in the 1928 Lord Mayor's parade.

The peoples' history

HISTORY, we were taught at school, is about kings and bishops and powerful magnates, wars and treaties. But that's only a small part of it. History is about ordinary people, living their lives in relative obscurity but playing their part in shaping the future of our nation.

Their stories are seldom told, yet they represent a world we can all relate to, one we live in and one that we observe changing. The tales told by our parents and grandparents of their childhood and early days are not fairy stories for children - they are the fabric of living history, and as vital to our understanding of earlier ages as any worthy historical tome.

In these pages we have endeavoured to bring you a flavour of bygone York and North Yorkshire, mainly told in the words of the people who were there - or through the recipients of that wisdom, their children and grandchildren.

These fascinating stories are a part of our history and there is a vital need to record them while we can. But, above all, we hope you find them a great read.

Martin Lacy

Credits

Yesterday Once More was written by Chris Titley, with the exception of the articles on Selby Toll Bridge, Selby Railway Bridge and Selby Abbey, which were written by Adrian Royles, and the History of Archbishop Holgate's School, which was written by Dan Roberts.

Most of the articles originally appeared in the Evening Press's weekly Yesterday Once More Column. Some were originally featured in various Evening Press Nostalgia publications.

Many of the pictures were provided by Evening Press readers. Others came from the paper's own library.

Yesterday Once More was edited by Martin Lacy

Cover picture: Hungate Mission at the turn of the century.

Backpiece: York's Parliament Street market, 1928.

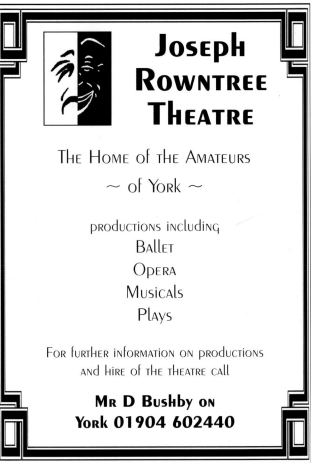

Residents of Millfield Road, York, celebrate the end of the Great War. Although the Armistice was signed in November , 1918, many street parties - like this one - were held over until the following summer.

Linking past and present

YORK archivist John Mitchell must have a sixth sense. The man in charge of the St Peter's School annals clearly has supernatural powers to uncover more information about the city's history.

On holiday, he was in a secondhand bookshop in Lewes, Sussex, when he was drawn to a book titled Memoirs of a Family 1822-1944.

Flicking through the book, by Robert Young, he discovered a chapter entitled Childhood in York 1914-24.

This details Mr Young's move from Preston to a new home in Clifton Terrace, York, and his upbringing at the time of the Great War. By a second coincidence, he went to St Olave's School, the prep school for St Peter's.

Naturally Mr Mitchell bought the book and added it to the extensive school archives.

Mr Young's memories of childhood add up to an evocative account of York 80 years ago.

"The war made some impact," he wrote. "I remember the scared face of cousin Win from New Zealand, who had been at Scarborough when the Germans shelled it from the sea.

"York began filling up with military hospitals and the walking wounded were clad in bright trousers, khaki jackets and red ties.

> **Childhood memories provide instant nostalgia and a link between the past and the present. Times long ago, often hazily glimpsed or remembered, connect us to our parents' and grandparents' eras - and open up a book on a world long disappeared.**

"Titled ladies assisted as nurses in the auxiliary homes. Mother shared in a tea bar at York Station, supplying drinks for troops.

"We were all told that the Kaiser had caused the war. He had fierce upturned military moustaches, not all that different from those of Kitchener, whose face gazed down from hoardings, urging Englishmen to enlist.

"The hoardings too had pictures of various types of friendly and enemy aeroplanes, for which we used to scan the sky, but it was the Zeppelins that dropped the bombs.

"These dirigible balloons on more than 30 occasions crossed the Yorkshire coast, and every time all the electric lights were switched off at the mains.

"There were not the sirens of the Second World

**Children gather round a house in Price's Lane, York after it was hit by a bomb
in a 1916 Zeppelin raid on the city.**

War, but a mass of searchlights criss-crossing the sky.

"When bombs actually dropped, we were hauled out of bed and spent the rest of the night under the family sideboard."

Mr Young recalled that there was "spy mania, even in York".

"Dad took a week in October 1914 or 15, before he used to take holidays harvesting. He was on a walk along the Roman wall with Arnold and Seebohm Rowntree when the three of them were arrested one evening in a pub by a village constable – presumably for spying on England's defences.

"Unfortunately for the constable, Arnold was Liberal Member of Parliament for the City of York."

The Minster played a big part in Mr Young's life for the 10 years he was resident in York.

"The Minster windows were slowly being removed and buried because the anti-aircraft gunfire and the occasional bombs were shaking out priceless pieces of medieval glass.

"It is sad to think that the whole process of removal and replacement had to take place at immense cost all over again for the Second World War.

"Two services I remember above all others. The first, early in the war, dedicated the tablet in the North Transept commemorating Admiral Craddock, who had sunk with all his ships at the Battle of Coronel.

"The second service was four years later, when on Armistice Day, November 11, 1918, most of the people of York flooded into the Minster to thank God for the end of the War.

"I have never heard 'O God Our Help In Ages Past' sung with such fervour."

Horses and carts, gas lights and knockers-up....

A QUARTER of a century ago, Sylvia Clayden sat down to record her childhood memories. She wanted to give her own children an insight into life in York at the beginning of the century. When she had finished, she had written a 25-page book full of fascinating detail and quirky reminiscences. It is a remarkable insight into times past.

Her daughter Jean Thompson, who lives in Carr Lane, Acomb, York said the book is not just about her late mother's life. "It's about the businesses, the prices - everything that was going on around the area."

Born Sylvia Sims in Aldwark, York in 1907, Mrs Clayden lived opposite the brewer John Joseph Hunt. "We were well used to horses and carts laden with hooped wooden beer barrels and the jovial men who when we asked them for a ride on the dray would promise one 'tomorrow' which never came," she wrote.

"Alarm clocks must have been a luxury or else of no avail to waken the sleeping workers, because we had 'knocker ups'. We who lived in Aldwark had a man or women who did the job.

"When she or he came to knock up, they used a long stick which was gently tapped against the window pane. The occupant had to assure the knocker up that they were awake.

"On one occasion the father of a large family including a young baby, who had kept him awake during the night, opened the bedroom window and emptied the contents of the chamber out and told the knocker up to clear off.

"He was blacklisted for a while and had to rely on the infants' wails to rouse him."

Mrs Clayden recalls the outbreak of World War One. Her father and uncle joined up and her two aunts left home to participate in war work. "Our household was getting smaller," she wrote.

"In our home was a gas light jet. I remember one night mother watched the gas flicker, this was their only warning of an air raid, quickly it went out and we were in utter darkness.

"We groped our way to a neighbour's house, she had a large cupboard under the stairs and she and her family were sitting in and were singing.

"One candle burned and we children didn't realise how lucky we'd been as people had been killed by a bomb as near as Peasholme Green.

"I saw the Zeppelin which did all the damage. To my mind it looked like a huge slow-moving silver bullet. It was eventually gunned down that night."

After the war, many children paid a penny to watch silent films at the Victoria Hall cinema which had entrances in Goodramgate and St Andrewgate.

"A man behind the red velvet curtains did the sound effects such as horses' hooves coming and going, train whistles and farmyard animals he could do to perfection. We only ever saw the top of his head but to us he was a man of magic".

Every year a Band of Hope gala was held with a march through Parliament Street. Mrs Clayden remembers plaiting the May Pole. Another annual event was the fair.

"Part of Peasholme Green was taken up with stalls which sold brandy snaps and sweets.

"A children's roundabout used to operate very near our door, rides cost one halfpenny and children used to sometimes cry to be taken off as the ride lasted longer than their little tummies could stand."

Christmases, days at Bedern Church School, the shops in Aldwark and Walmgate: they are all captured in her book for posterity.

Mrs Clayden finished by saying: "For my part I think we had the happiest period. Only time will prove me right or wrong."

Frightening visitors with 'the tippler'....

RETIRED British Rail manager Arnold Pygott is now in his late 80s but age has not dimmed his memories of growing up in York between the wars. He has written an evocative account of life from the time of the First World War to the start of the Second.

"I believe that 1939 saw the end of an era," he writes. "The period of the Second World War was in many respects a social desert; life stood still, but afterwards a whole new world emerged."

Mr Pygott, who now lives in Haxby, was born in a house facing York racecourse and grew up in the Holgate district.

"The main feature of the house was the outside toilet, operating on the tippler system, which was fed by water from the kitchen sink and the bathroom.

"The tippler was large, heavy, and made of glazed pot situated about three feet below the toilet seat.

"It operated with a tremendous noise and a rush of water.

"Occasionally when we had visitors, unaware of this scientific wonder, it was not unknown for my brothers to turn on all the taps - it was a thunderous noise and quite an experience."

During his lifetime, he has seen incredible scientific advances, from the moon landings to micro-computers. But the two that made the most impression on him were the introduction of electricity and the radio.

"The Electricity Company said they would install electric lighting if seven people in the street would agree to it.

"This duly occurred and wonder of wonders, at the touch of a switch on came a beautiful light.

"Prior to this, we took a candle upstairs and lit a small gas jet in the bedroom.

"Gas gave a nice soft light, but was not very convenient; mantles were always breaking and much time was spent cleaning the fittings which became smoked up."

He was a pupil at Priory Street Higher Grade School during the Great War.

He writes: "As children we were quite unaware of the terrible carnage and conditions on the Western Front, although as I grew a bit older I remember reading column after column of deaths in the paper.

"We were more concerned with the romantic side of war. Soldiers were bivouacked on the Knavesmire and even now I can catch the savoury smells coming from their billycans.

"Sometimes a battalion of infantry would be doing a route march led by an officer on a horse.

"This would thrill us more than anything, even without a band!"

Despite the austerity of the war years Mr Pygott said that "life as a small child was full of sparkle".

"There were always exciting things to do. Picnics at Nether Poppleton by the river where the Boy Scouts used to camp, or cricket on Hob Moor, where on a summer's day the air was full of the sight and sound of skylarks.

"In the autumn we were gathering horse chestnuts on Boroughbridge Road, and playing conkers and marbles.

"There was also the hoop or booler as it was called. Wherever we went, whether running errands or just playing, the faithful booler accompanied us."

Getting around as he grew older was no problem.

"In my youth electric trams were an accepted part of the landscape. My last recollection of the fare was two pence (old money) anywhere.

"In the early days there was no cover on the top deck and in wet weather (when more people used them) everybody tried to cram inside.

"Horses were very much in evidence during the early part of the century. York Fire Brigade was still using horses in the early part of the century and I can well remember seeing them racing up Acomb Road with two horses in full charge."

Mr Pygott left Nunthorpe School in 1927 and started work at London and North Eastern Railway company, earning £1 10 shillings a week.

"In the Thirties cinemas were having their most prosperous time; there were in York, I think, six cinemas and at the weekend people queued to get in.

"Originally the New Street cinema had been an old chapel with shuttered windows. These were closed to keep the light out.

"The performances were at fixed times and when they commenced a bell was rung to warn

The early 1930s when getting from Acomb to York meant walking or taking the electric tram.

people that lights were going out.

"Coney Street cinema (now the site of Woolworth's) was the only one with a café attached. It was a popular gathering place for young people and one could sit all evening with one cup of coffee, price 4d.

"My first experience of going to a cinema was when my older friends took me to the Electric in Fossgate.

"A special Saturday was put on for children. The charge was 2d which was placed in a bucket at the door and for which we were regaled with episodes of Pearl White the intrepid detective (to be continued next week) and the Clutching Hand with somebody murdered every week."

Dancing their way into the limelight....

COUNTLESS thousands of children have been taught dance by Isobel Dunn. Yet somehow when she goes through her photograph album she can put a name to every face. How does she remember them all? "I don't know – I just do," she said at her home in Scarcroft Road, York.

A good number of her pupils have gone on to become professional dancers.

Michael Pink a student 25 years ago, is now the assistant artistic director of the Northern Ballet.

Christopher Ackrill went on to join the Malmo Ballet Company and is now with the Hanover ballet in Germany, Dawn Sutton and Wendy Dawson are both with the Scottish ballet and Julie Pickering is a member of the Northern Ballet.

There are many more who make their living from dancing around the world, some on cruise liners, some as booking agents for dance companies; and there are those who just enjoy dance as a hobby. They all share a love of this art immeasurably enhanced by Miss Dunn. Isobel Dunn has dominated York's dance scene for half a century.

Mr Pink vividly remembers when he first started lessons with her.

"She scared the living daylights out of me.

"She's a good disciplinarian which is what our profession is about. You have got to be firm in the right way.

"She treated me in the way that got me through to the ballet school. She's a cornerstone of York."

Beryl Bunn has been involved in the Isobel Dunn School of Dancing since she met its founder while working on set designs at York Theatre Royal in 1959.

She said: "The girls who go to stage school in London, they come back and say 'We're glad Miss Dunn was like she was, because when we go to

York dance teacher Isobel Dunn with some of her 1990s pupils.

state school and get told off it doesn't hurt us'."

"I am tough, full stop," Miss Dunn said. "I have to do it my way. Sometimes students get frustrated because they can't do it.

"You have to get them over that line, even by getting cross."

As a girl, Miss Dunn would put on shows in the attic of her father's grocery store on Lawrence Street, York. "We would perform plays and it cost two cigarette cards to get in.

"If we played games, I would always be the school teacher – the boss."

The former nurse and Tiller girl began teaching children to dance while working at Rowntrees: the packing and stores department sponsored her first shows. Then she took it up full time, qualifying for all the Royal Academy teaching certificates.

Children's general classes on a Saturday cost one shilling, and private lessons in "tap, ballet, limbering, musical comedy, acrobatic" cost double.

Her dance studio was the attic room above her father's shop. In October 1945, she put on her first show in the Co-operative Hall, Hull Road, York, with the first Dance Flash staged the following year.

One of the pupils in the 1945 'Display of Dancing' was Betty Daltry. Now Mrs Smeeton, Betty, remembers those days with extreme fondness.

"I loved it – ballet, tap, the whole spectrum," she said. "Miss Dunn was strict but fair. We did as we were told, or we tried to!

"She was such a good teacher right from the start, with determination and dedication, and she got results. She was great fun and I enjoyed every minute of it."

In the austere, post war years when Miss Dunn began to teach, resources were scarce. "You had to have pink ballet shoes for the exams," she said.

"I painted mine with Chinese lacquer – every time you stood in filth your feet stuck together."

Mothers of the pupils improvised costumes using patchwork for dresses and cardboard for hats.

When she put on Dance Flash at the old SS Empire – now the Grand Opera House – there was not enough dressing room space.

"The children used to dress in The Castle Pub opposite the theatre. We had to have a policeman who would stop all the traffic and get them across when it was time to go on."

Miss Dunn moved from Lawrence Street to a studio above Mr Beaumont's bakery in Walmgate, York before taking over her current premises in Market Street, above the Early Learning Centre.

It takes grit to develop into a dancer, Miss Dunn said.

"There's the physical build – God sends that.

"Then it's determination all the way, to flog it and flog it and flog it, until you have got it.

"Nowadays children don't understand how to learn. It isn't that they're not keen, they just

York dance teacher Isobel Dunn in the 1940s.

don't know how to learn."

After more than 50 years, Miss Dunn is now teaching different generations of the same families. But she has dismissed all thoughts of retirement.

"I thought I would retire, then I thought 'what would I do with all that time?'"

The boys of the Blues and Greys....

I T started with a group of 30 boys. In the intervening years, St Chad's Greys Scout Group has provided enjoyment and education for hundreds of youngsters in York. In May 1926, the group was established by its first group Scout leader, the Reverend George Boddy, assisted by Edward Lang.

The name 'Greys' derived from the colour of the uniform jersey and the neckerchief, an ingenious piece of clothing comprising a black triangle folded over a white triangle. This formed a sling and a triangular bandage, so each Scout could live up to the famous motto: "Be Prepared."

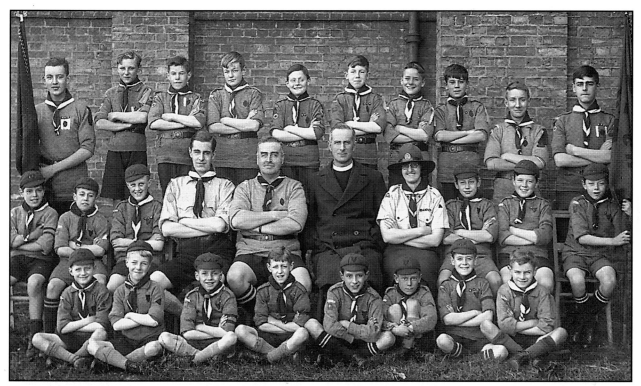

The 1st Cub Pack of the St Chad's Greys pictured outside St Chad's Church, Campelshon Road, York, in the 1920s. The adults in the middle row are, left to right, Edward Lang, Mr Dupe, the Reverend George Boddy and Gladys Roche.

At this time, there was also a second pack of Cubs who met in the Mission Hall on South Bank Avenue, now a glass workshop. The Cub Scout leader of the first pack was Mrs Roach and her counterpart in the second pack was Lily Lonsdale.

In 1933, the packs merged. By this time Mr Lang had become group Scout leader, Mr Boddy having moved to another parish.

The group flourished, entering many York competitions and enjoying camping trips across Yorkshire and in the Lake District.

They also went further afield, taking part in world Scouting jamborees.

Bert Jessop, of Reginald Grove, York, has unrivalled knowledge of Scouting in this area.

He started as a Cub in 1932 at St Chad's and became assistant Scout leader when Leslie Goodrick took over the group. Mr Lang had left to become a youth leader in Cambridge.

Mr Jessop was appointed district commissioner York South then city commissioner, and was deputy county commissioner when he retired at 65 in 1990.

Mr Jessop, now president of the group, recalled how the Greys vacated St Chad's Parish Hall during the Second World War to make room for the Army. This made fundraising difficult as the hall had always been used for dances, which paid for many activities, uniform and equipment.

When they decided to begin a Scout group band, they chose the English Martyrs Hall in Blossom Street, next to the Odeon Cinema to host weekly fundraising dances.

Five mothers were escorted there in the blackout to serve refreshments.

After 18 months, they had enough money to buy the instruments and the well known St Chad's Greys Band was born.

Although it returned to the parish hall when the war ended, the success of the group meant it was outgrowing this accommodation. The hall was sold – it is now St Clement's Working Men's Club – and land at the rear of the church was secured for a purpose-built Scout headquarters.

In 1957, the grand opening ceremony took place with the Lord Lieutenant of North Yorkshire and president of the county Scout movement, Sir William Worsley, guest of honour.

The group went from strength to strength. Today there are two Beaver units, two Cub packs, one Scout troop and one Venture Scout unit.

Its 70th anniversary was marked with a reunion dinner dance at the Gimcrack Rooms, York Racecourse, with one former member travelling from Canada to take part.

The Greys has provided three Church canons – the late Allen Batty, Stanley Nicholls and Ron Metcalfe, a canon at York Minster.

Mr Jessop said: "Many lads who enjoyed their time in the Greys have made successes in their careers and are proud to have been part of it."

Happy days in Hungate: terrible housing conditions and frequent floodings couldn't wipe the smiles from these cheerful 30s residents of York's worst slum area.

Community spirit made life in the slums bearable

IF you stand with your back to Stonebow House, which many would argue is the best thing to do to the building, you face what was one of the most poverty-ravaged slums in York. Hungate today is an unspectacular city centre street. But before the war, the name Hungate referred to an area cramped with filthy tenements.

This grimy warren housed hundreds of families but only just. One Hungate child in four died before their first birthday in 1900. Its eventual fate was to be condemned as unfit for human habitation and demolished.

There was an incredible community spirit in spite of, or perhaps inspired by, the terrible conditions, however. The picture at the top of this page, taken in 1933, sums it up.

On the far left is Richard Butterworth, known as Dick or Dickie, and next to him is brother John, a painter and decorator. They are standing outside the house belonging to their parents William and Annie in Westley Place, Hungate. The boy without the cap is George Ellis, who still lives in York, and the other thought to be Jammy or Ginger Richmond, who left the city some years ago.

On the left of the two girls is Madge Lightfoot, later to become Madge Carter; and on her left is Mary Hall, née Melia.

Hungate in the 1920s and the 1930s was a self-

Casual visitors to York are immediately struck by the quality of the buildings - fine Medieval halls, wonderful timbered houses of Tudor and Stuart times, elegant Georgian mansions and solid and imposing Victorian homes and offices. Even the leafy suburbs impress. But times not so long ago were very different. Economic depression in the city at the end of the last century and the beginning of this created appalling slums areas and squalid conditions. Yet despite the lack of amenities - one tap for half a dozen houses, toilets at the end of the street, damp and dirt - Evening Press readers recall happy days when neighbours were friends and community spirit meant a helping hand for those in need.

The Woolpack Inn (above) was the focal point of York's Hungate area, which consisted of tatty tenements and small yards (left) where amenities were very basic but community spirit strong.

help community. In the days before the welfare state, people relied on each other; neighbourliness was not a bonus, it was a necessity. Madge Carter said of her childhood: "Everybody knew everybody, everybody helped everybody."

Ron Pearson was born in nearby St Saviourgate in 1915. He remembered: "One of the most striking memories was the kids running around in no shoes, with their backsides hanging out. We were discouraged from going down there."

Gladys Raftree's late husband Jackie lived in Hungate. "I used to sit on the wall with him along by the Foss," she recalled. "We used to go down by St Saviourgate – it was a lot of wasteground then."

Most of the men and women in Hungate were employed at Leetham's Mill, now Rowntree Wharf; or the gasworks, whose site is occupied by Sainsbury's today; or at local slaughterhouses. But their regular wage was only enough to afford the most basic living conditions.

One of the focal points of Hungate was the Woolpack pub. It had its own rugby team who played every Saturday. After the slum clearances, the team transferred to the former Imperial Hotel, Clifton, York.

The coach, dressed in an overcoat in our picture (below) from the 1936/37 season, was Harry Dale. His grandson Brian Dale said two of Harry's sons (he had seven sons and four daughters) played professionally for York. Mr Dale was also the Evening Press correspondent known as the Rugby Leaguer, writing match reports for the newspaper.

The 1936 team was a family affair. Peewee and George Thorpe were brothers, and Albert Metcalfe and Sammy Bardy were cousins.

A marvellous book, Rich In All But Money, chronicles Hungate in the words of its residents from the beginning of the century until the slum housing was demolished in 1938.

Published by the Archaeological Resource Centre in St Saviourgate, York, it tells the story of the parish through the words of those born and brought up there. Author Van Wilson, with the help of the York Oral History Project, has captured both the harshness of the environment and the soul of the people.

"No-one believed they lived in such a terrible state and I must say the people were pretty charming although they were suffering," recalls Dorothy Reynolds in the book. She used to live in the relative affluence of St Saviourgate.

"In the olden days York was known as the three Ps - poor, proud and pretty. Under the pretty side was the seamy side."

"There was one cold tap and if you wanted water to get a bath, you used to boil it," said George Squire of his first home, in Haver Lane.

"I think the worst thing of all was the black-locks (beetles). When you turned the light out and if you came round and struck a match, the floor would be covered in blacklocks. You could smell them."

The memories of Rene Sheard, who died recently, are included in the book. Her recollections of childhood are a stark reminder of how dramatically things have improved over the last 70 years.

"When I was a kid, I was always with my dad and we used to go down to the cellar to relieve the mice from the traps. There was tons of mice there.

"And of course they were all dead, and I used to put all these dead mice, every morning, into me doll's pram, and if it was a wet day I used to wrap 'em up in Wright's polony skin and they were me babies." Yet the crippling poverty did nothing to diminish the pride, decency and fellowship that thrived in Hungate. The book evokes a world of best rooms, mothers baking bread on the York Range, policemen who knew the names of all the children in their patch, and doctors who dished out wide-ranging advice along with the medicine.

Today's teachers might be forgiven for a wistful sigh on reading about the life of one master, Mr Golledge who taught at Haughton School, St Saviourgate. Mrs Sheard, the daughter of a publican, said: "He used to come in at dinner time when the school was empty, stand against the bar - his usual order a double whisky and a bot-

The Woolpack Rugby League team, 1936/7

The end is near: a rag and bone man trundles away his treasures from the empty houses in Redness Street, Layerthorpe, York, in 1962 shortly before demolition.

tle of Guinness - and that was it … my education was paid through that bill, no cash passed over."

When the Hungate residents were rehoused in clean, modern council accommodation many of them soon began to miss this strong sense of community. Van Wilson said: "A lot of the people that we have spoken to said that since they got to the new council housing, with electric lights and indoor toilets, they wanted to go back.

"They missed the community spirit, when there were always people to turn to."

Andy Waudby, born in Hungate in 1921, sums up that spirit in the book. He described the area's residents as 'wonderful people'.

"They'll give you anything. Anybody knocked at that door and wanted a cup of tea or something to eat, we'd share it with 'em straight away. This is Hungate people. That makes us so proud. Because we feel for others".

It was certainly never a prosperous area. In the book Dick Caplin, of Heworth, remembers conditions in his house in Rosemary Yard.

"We were damp and when we used to go out at night-time and then put the light on, the beetles would be running out of all corners. There was one tap in the yard for six families."

"Half an egg, that's what we had," Joyce Burnett, said recalling childhood mealtimes. "And my dad used to do toasted cheese.

"He used to put milk in and we had the gravy, we didn't have the cheese. I can remember my mother saying, 'you've got the goodness in the gravy, get that down you.'"

Children would be sent out to work to help the family finances. Stan Cowen, became an errand boy for Gaythorpe's butchers, next to the Five Lions in Walmgate, when he was 11.

He tells in the book of working from 5.30pm to 8.30pm on a Friday night and 8.30am to 9pm on a Saturday.

"The man I worked for used to take snuff. And I'd go to the shop for his snuff and for tobacco.

"You could get the flake tobacco loose, but mostly it was like coils of rope. And he would have on the counter a small wooden block like a cheese slicer with a knife on it and a blade. And he'd cut what they called thin twist or thick twist."

Life was tough in a former Viking settlement

SQUEEZED between Peasholme Green and Heworth is the York suburb of Layerthorpe. Now a bustling neighbourhood where family homes jostle alongside retailing and industry, it began as a stand-alone village and has a long and fascinating history, inspiring

The changing face of Layerthorpe: This painting (above) of the medieval bridge (demolished in 1829) paints a scene of rural bliss - a far cry from the grim housing of post war Layerthorpe (below) when the River Foss was a source of danger not a leisure resource.

Avril Webster to write Looking Back At Layerthorpe: a York Suburb, after talking to her father-in-law, Ernest Webster.

"He gave me some old family photographs," Avril writes in the introduction, "and told me many interesting tales, some sad, some funny anecdotes and incidents."

The recollections of Mr Webster, now in his nineties, inspired her to compile what is a meticulously researched book about the suburb. Avril, who carried out her research over three years, said: "I decided to write it now because the area is changing so much."

The book traces Layerthorpe back to Viking times, with Layer originating either from "leger" - a burial place – or "laira/leira", meaning a place of clay. Thorpe simply means "settlement".

And the Evening Press has reported a heated debate over the correct name for the bridge which leads to the suburb.

According to Avril's findings Layerthorpe Bridge was first mentioned in 1200, and until the 19th century it was always known by that name or as Layerthorpe Postern Bridge. The first bridge and postern was demolished in 1829 by York Corporation after falling into disrepair. Stone and bricks from the original structure were used in the new, wider version, initially called Peasholme Green Bridge.

This was an unpopular name, however, and it was soon called Layerthorpe Bridge again. So there you are.

The industrialisation of York saw the expansion of Layerthorpe, with new streets built quickly and often poorly: flooding from the Foss was a regular hazard.

Sanitary conditions were awful. Slaughterhouses and stables were built next door to the poorest houses. In 1884, more than 40 cases of typhoid were recorded in the area.

Layerthorpe was considered one of the poorer areas of York in the early part of the 20th century.

Family feuds and drink often led to fights: police patrolled in twos and on one occasion an officer was thrown over Layerthorpe Bridge into the Foss.

It is the personal reminiscences included in the book, more than the detailed history, that make it such a worthwhile read.

The recollections of sisters Elsie Johnson, Olive King and Minnie White bring Layerthorpe in the 1920s and the 1930s back to life.

"They recalled the chemist, Mr Newey, with his shop on the main road near Layerthorpe Buildings," Avril writes. "He wore a black pillbox hat and they thought as children that the sign W Newey, MPS meant 'Mr Newey makes people sick'…

"They would often run errands for old ladies in their street. One lady would send them to the George IV public house for her daily jug of beer, but always put the red hot poker in it before drinking."

Stories abound about the John Bull, first mentioned as a public house in the street directories of the 1830s and demolished in 1995 to make way for an extension to the Turnbulls Mazda motor showroom.

At closing time one night in the 1930s, someone suggested a diving competition.

"Five or six men in their underpants stood on the bridge and at the count of three had to dive. Bull Kirby, the local strong man, was the only one to dive – the others got dressed.

"Poor Bull came out of the river dripping wet and cussing, but he won a few pints that night."

Other memories recounted include Bilton Street School being damaged by Second World War bombs; the Frog Hall pub and its many social activities; York Boys' Club and its leader in the 1950s, William Ogilvie, known as "Skip".

The area changed dramatically after the compulsory purchase orders and demolition in 1959 and 1960.

Changing face of the village that became a suburb

ACOMB is much more than a suburb of the city of York. With a population now said to be larger than that of Bridlington, it retains a character of its own. But it has changed dramatically in the last 50 years.

Local historian Geoff Hodgson discovered how times had altered the area when he began researching it for his talk An Outsider's View Of Acomb, Its Buildings and People, in the Not So Long Ago series at York Library.

He originally hails from Holgate and now lives in Rufforth. But he has clear memories of the Acomb of 50 years ago - carefree expeditions to the brick ponds, armed with fishing net, jam jar and string.

The trophies he brought back were minnows, sticklebacks, the occasional newt and masses of frogspawn.

"There were large brick ponds in the area now covered by the Edmund Wilson Baths on Thanet Road," he said.

As the proud owner of a Hornby train set at the beginning of the war, he made accessories by baking excavated clay in the oven.

He recalls visits to Acomb Church Hall to hear the Reverend G Bramwell Evans, better known as 'Romany' of BBC Radio's Children's Hour. Mr Bramwell Evans illustrated his talks with large-scale charcoal drawings done on the spot.

Acomb ceased being a village and became part of York in 1937. Holgate was swallowed up by the city in 1884.

"I think most Acomb people will say it's lost the

Acomb in the 1920s - still a farming village before it was swallowed up as a suburb of York.

THESE young boys are pictured in Front Street, Acomb, York, waiting for a charabanc outing. They are standing outside the Methodist church in this turn-of-the-century photograph, which is now the Ebor Carpet Warehouse. Older Acomb residents will remember the shop next door, Baker and Till's grocers shop, which displayed a Rowntree's sign and sold Fry's pure cocoa. The church, which moved to newer premises over the road, was sold in 1960 years ago to a fireplace retailer. It then became Bond Removals, and was the base for many years for Dennis Yorke's, the rug firm.

feeling of a village," Mr Hodgson said.

"When you have 25,000 people concentrated in that community, you have to look reasonably carefully to see signs of the old village."

Acomb used to be a farming area. "It was an agricultural community. There were at least five farms, mostly on Front Street.

"I am told that on the day that Acomb came into York, four of its farms moved all their stock to villages further away from York because all their grassing ground would eventually be swallowed up by housing estate."

Today, the line separating Acomb and Holgate is often blurred - although not by those who live there. But Mr Hodgson believes there are key differences between the two.

"I think Acomb has a more obvious village centre than Holgate. The changes occurred in Holgate over 50 years earlier. It became incorporated in the 1880s." The older housing in Holgate reflects that, he said. Acomb developed mainly from the 1930s onwards. "To my mind the older housing has more character."

Mr Hodson's talk chronicled Acomb from its beginning as an ancient settlement, concentrating on changes that have occurred within living memory.

Going, going...Walmgate's once-busy shopping area is condemned (above) in the 1960s and demolished (below) at the end of the decade.

Pubs, home-made remedies, and cow wallopers....

WALMGATE is one of York's more distinctive streets, boasting a varied mix of shops, cafes and housing. It was the same only more so in the first half of the century. But there is little still standing that residents from those days would immediately recognise.

Walmgate was a bustling community. The street was packed with shops: Matty Myers, newsagent and tobacconist; Parker's and Beaumont's, the bakeries, selling penny hot cakes; Ellerker the butchers and Haythornes, the pawn shop, which was always busy.

Many of the residents were very poor. Some of the worst poverty was among the Irish labourers' families. To avoid doctors' bills people would consult Thomas Batty, the chemist situated near the bar, about their ailments.

On cattle market day, a familiar sight would be the cows being herded along the street with the 'cow wallopers' leading them down.

Walmgate also boasted an infamous parade of pubs: the Admiral Hawke, the Black Bull, the Spotted Dog, two Malt Shovels, the Brewer's Arms, the Ham and Firkin, Shakespeare's Tap... the list goes on. At one stage, every other building was said to be a pub.

Walmgate was a hive of industry. Its manufacturing industry included Bellerby's match mill and George Eastwood tool makers. There was a cattle market through Walmgate bar and the brewery off George Street.

The Navigation Road glassworks was another important factory. But by the 1950s much of Navigation Road was just waste ground where

Margaret Street, Walmgate - condemned in 1954 and demolished to make way for modern flats.

children played. Today it boasts a modern housing development.

Other Walmgate traders included the Shaftoe family, who ran a profitable business in Barleycorn Yard making clay tobacco pipes, a great favourite with the Irish community.

Thomlinson-Walker designed and built the ironwork for many York buildings, as well as constructing the gates of the Royal Botanical Gardens in Mauritius and the railings outside the British Museum in London. And there was Poad's, the grain and seed merchants.

The list of Walmgate shops was long. It included Crow's Butchers, Cambage's greengrocers, and Lovick's - one of six drapers in the street.

Harry Lovick, now in his 70s, remembered working there. "When I was a little boy, ladies in Walmgate never wore overcoats, all they wore was a black shawl which they'd put over their heads and round their shoulders.

"We sold our cheapest men's cap for one shilling, five pence in new money and our most expensive cap was half a crown."

Ina Paterson recorded her Walmgate memories in an interview with York historian Van Wilson. Ina recalled the life of her great-grandmother Ann Elizabeth Oxtoby.

Better known as Macy Ann, she married William Linfoot Boulton. Mrs Boulton was a midwife and Navigation School caretaker who lived in Walmgate in the 1880s. She died in 1908.

Macy cared for many of the wives of Irish itinerant labourers. She would be woken up in the night by the policeman and taken over to one of the lodging houses to deliver babies.

She was renowned for her home-made remedies. Mrs Paterson: "She used to make her own ointment which people used to come from quite a wide area to buy, in little pots for sixpence.

"My mother, when she was young, stayed with her grandma and she had to help with chores.

One of her chores was to go to Crow's pork butchers just within Walmgate Bar.

"She would go and buy six pennyworth of pig's leaf which is the inner membrane of the pig's ear. Her grandma would put it in the oven in a baking dish and render it down and it made a thick white fat.

"On the outhouse roof in the schoolyard grew a lot of sempra vivum, a succulent plant in a rosette shape which grows copiously in the Mediterranean on roofs and walls.

"In York it is called 'ooselak', which is dialect for houseleaf. This had a cactus type leaf and she gathered it and crushed it in the pestle and mortar and added the juicy remains to this white pig fat.

"It made a very good ointment for skin troubles and nappy rash. And it worked. You had your own remedies in those days, because you couldn't afford to run to the doctor every five minutes.

"My mother used to get thick biscuits, like ship's biscuits, from Slater's tea stall at the top of Fossgate.

"Her grandmother scalded them with hot water, drained off any surplus moisture, added sugar and then boiled milk and this was made up for babies who were not feeding very well or if their mothers hadn't hardly any milk, then this was spooned or bottle fed to them.

"There were no flavoured baby foods then.

"At Christmas she always made a big bowl of 'frumerty'. This was creeded wheat (steeped in water for ages, like the old fashioned way of making rice pudding) added to milk, sugar, nutmeg and other spices.

"Perhaps in some areas they laced it with a bit of spirit."

YORKSHIRE Fire and Life Insurance Company.
ESTABLISHED AT YORK, 1824.

GENERAL ACCIDENT LIFE

2 Rougier Street, York

Tel 01904 628982

I N 1824 the first meeting of the YORKSHIRE FIRE & LIFE Insurance company took place at 'The York Tavern' in St Helen's Square, now occupied by Betty's.

Over the next 100 years a number of acquisitions and name changes took place, then in 1925 the company became a subsidiary of GENERAL ACCIDENT FIRE & LIFE ASSURANCE COMPANY.

General Life took over the YORKSHIRE INSURANCE COMPANY in 1967/8, and the company went through a series of name changes finally resulting in GENERAL ACCIDENT LIFE.

To this day GENERAL ACCIDENT LIFE continues to develop in York. The recent opening of its new headquarters in Wellington Row and the acquisition of pensions specialists Provident Mutual heralded a new chapter in its already successful story bringing continual employment opportunities, business prosperity and even greater recognition to the city as a major business capital.

Early days: pupils - and teacher - at Park Grove School, York, in 1895, the year the school opened.

Best years of our lives?

PARK Grove County Primary School is loved by its pupils, their parents and the community at whose heart it has stood for more than 100 years. That was clear from the almost tangible sense of loss in The Groves the morning after a devastating fire gutted the Victorian building in 1997.

Such heartbreak was not felt only by the present generation of children and their families. Those who attended the school many years, even decades, ago were also affected by the destruction of the school.

Several former pupils contacted the Evening Press after the fire. They wanted to express their gratitude to a school that gave them such a good start in life, their anguish at the fire and their hope that it can bounce back from this terrible blow.

Park Grove was opened in 1895, and a reader's historic photograph (above) shows one of its very first classes.

This picture of an infant class, taken by The Elementary Schools Photographic Company, was brought in by Ellen Lockwood, of Priory Street, York.

It is not dated. But Mrs Lockwood's father Joe Long can be seen on the far right of the second row from the back.

He looks about five years old. As he was born in

> **Schooldays are reckoned to be the best years of our lives - and judging by the memories recorded in this chapter, they certainly were. Schools have changed greatly during the course of the century, with many readers bemoaning the lack of discipline in modern schools and praising the quality of teachers of yesteryear. More than anything, readers recall just how much fun they had at school.**

York in 1890, that means the picture must be one of the first ever taken at the school. Next to Joe on the picture is his brother, Fred Long, who was a year younger.

Little can be seen of the building, which would have been brand new of course, except for a window and some brickwork behind the group of children.

Mrs Lockwood, said that her father had very fond memories of the place. "He said it was a marvellous school.

"He was quite clever. If he had stayed on at

school he would have done really well, but he had to go out to work."

Her father became a driver, and was a chauffeur during the war. "He said he had the oldest driving licence in England."

Fred Long became a journalist with news agency Reuters. But the two brothers were by no means the only members of the family to go to Park Grove, Mrs Lockwood points out.

"My father had lots of brothers and sisters. They would all have gone to Park Grove as they lived off Monkgate, in Agar Street and then Jewbury where Sainsbury's is now."

Considering Mr Long's love for the school, it is perhaps not surprising that he chose to send Ellen there when she reached primary age.

A generation on, and the school's magic was still working. "It was a really lovely school, with nice teachers," she remembered.

"I always remember the windows were quite high, and we used to have bunches of flowers in the window.

"When I was a little girl, the teacher used to give me bunches of flowers from the window on Friday.

"They always had sweets for you as well."

The recent fire was not the first time pupils were forced out of their classrooms, as Madge Turner, of York, recalls.

"During the 1914-18 War, the school was occupied by the Army and pupils had to attend Monkgate Chapel," she said.

"The juniors were downstairs and the seniors were upstairs. All the kiddies who had fathers in the Army were given boxes of chocolates."

Mrs Turner, who later was amongst the first group to be given the status of Freewomen of York, added: "When the Army vacated the site towards the end of the War the pupils, including myself had to carry piles of books from Monkgate to the school along Huntington Road."

Brenda Batty's memories date from after the Second World War. She was a pupil from 1947 to 1953.

She said: "It seems like yesterday when we used to have a nap in the afternoon on metal beds and a pink blanket.

"In winter we used to have to warm our milk as it was all iced up. As we progressed to the top class in the infants we had to help the smaller children tie their shoelaces."

It was a strict place but happy too, Mrs Batty, of Heworth, York, said. "I remember one corner of the playground was our palace. We had to pretend to be on horseback as princes and princesses.

"I know it was old fashioned but I don't think that deteriorated at all from the quality of the teaching."

We were also contacted by a former teacher at Park Grove school. John Found, of Scarborough, trained at St John's College, Lord Mayor's Walk, before joining the staff at the Dudley Street school in September 1961.

The headteacher then was John Spooner. "He gave me much help and advice and was to

Teachers at Park Grove School in 1962: men (from left) Mr Robinson, Mr Scaife, Mr Found and headmaster Mr Spooner. Women (from left) Mrs Clark, Mrs Littlewood, Miss Thompson, Miss Corbett and Mrs Holmes.

remain a good friend over the years," Mr Found said.

"He was succeeded by his deputy, Mr JJ 'Robbie' Robinson, and the school developed into one of the happiest schools I ever worked in.

"The staff was splendid, the parents ever supportive and although many of the children came from the humblest of backgrounds, there was always a happy, hard working atmosphere about the place."

Mr Found also met his wife, Judith Corbett, at Park Grove. She was on the staff, and they married in 1963.

He went on to become head of a village school near Scarborough. "However, my years at 'Parkie' were undoubtedly the most rewarding of all," he said.

For generations, Park Grove has provide a happy, secure environment for its children. Everyone who contacted the Evening Press expressed their optimism that the marvellous spirit at the school would be enough to see it bounce back from the fire.

And many readers will agree with the sentiments of Mrs Batty, who said: "I do hope it will be rebuilt - although we all know it will never be the same."

Study, sports days and stuffed seabirds!

THERE are 125 pupils on this spectacular school photograph (below) and all of them are looking at the camera. Quite an achievement, but students of Haughton School, St Saviourgate, York, were obviously made of stern stuff in 1927, when this picture was taken.

The headmaster, George Henry Golledge, complete with mortar board and bow tie, is at the centre of the second row.

On his right is another master, Mr C A Heron, later to become head, and next to him, again in mortar board and sporting a splendid moustache, is the deputy, the Reverend G C Beech, vicar of St Martin-cum-Gregory in York.

It was common in those days for the sons of teachers to go into the profession, and George Golledge's son Reginald is in the stripy tie next to Mr Beech. His wife is on the headmaster's left, holding a dog.

Haughton School was founded in 1770 by philanthropist Captain William Haughton. He cajoled local clergymen into helping to teach a group of about 40 poor boys.

Captain Haughton was a dancing master in the city who eventually died in London but was buried in York.

This picture was taken at the school's sports ground, St Oswald's Road, Fulford. Children were taken there by what were, at that time, York's new buses.

Pupils from infant age and over were taught at Haughton. Girls wore black gymslips with a red sash and green, cloche hats. Boys had green blazers with gilt edging.

The uniform sported the school badge, a green shield with gold border and a red cross. The school's Latin motto, Finis Coronat Opus, means The End Crowns The Work.

Unusually for this time, some students, aged 16 and 17, remained at Haughton School. They were often due to follow into their father's business and stayed at school for preparatory tuition.

There was a mixture of boarders and day pupils, with sleeping accommodation for the girls separated from the boys' quarters by the road.

Lessons were very traditional, with former pupils still able to decline their Latin verbs to this day. Young children would be taught algebra and fractions and French was the second language.

With cricket in the summer and football in the winter, sport for the boys was also traditional.

Additionally there was the Haughton School "marathon" – where pupils ran the full length of Knavesmire racecourse and the winner was awarded a trophy.

The school museum was a source of fascination for students. It featured a propeller, shot through with bullet holes and with half a blade missing, as a memorial for all the Old Boys who had died in the Great War.

A collection of every British seabird, stuffed and

Haughton School sports days, 1927.

mounted in glass cases, was bequeathed to the museum by a former pupil.

London firm Panora Ltd took this splendid photograph, which was for the front of a brochure promoting the school. More than a hundred pupils were involved, about a third to a half of the school roll.

It was framed by J A Jacques, whose workshop used to be next to the entrance of Craven's Sweet Factory, where the Jorvik Viking Centre is now, in Coppergate, York.

Haughton School closed in 1955, 185 years after opening. Mr Heron was headmaster having taken over in 1938 from Mr Golledge who was in charge for 40 years.

Still in the school at the time of its closure was a desk which carried the inscription: "The Rev John Overton, headmaster, took possession of this desk in January 1828."

T-squared kept the girls in line

WHEN York College For Girls closed in 1997, it was the end of an educational era. Thousands of girls had been taught at the Petergate school in its near-90 year history. Former students across the city shared in the sadness of the present generation of pupils when its classrooms fell silent forever.

York College for Girls opened on Friday January 24, 1908. This picture below shows the first headmistress Miss E Ellett and the original intake of pupils.

As well as the 30 or so girls, there are also a few kindergarten boys, including six-year-old James Swift. His father, the Blake Street solicitor HL Swift, was secretary to the governors, and in this role placed the first advertisement for the school.

Dating from the York Herald of January 15, 1908, it announced the opening of "a first class girls' school and kindergarten".

Next to Miss Ellett are the four first members of staff including the second mistress Miss Addison: the Addison Library in the school was named in commemoration of her following her early death in 1928.

By the end of 1908 there were 61 pupils on the roll, rising to 132 two years later.

The occupations of most parents in the early days are recorded in the school's archives, which are administered by Eleanor Reader – a pupil from 1922-1931.

Nine of the fathers of the 1908 intake were Church of England clergy; the rest included doctors, bankers, merchants, lawyers, teachers, civil engineers, farmers, a landed proprietor, an actuary, an Army officer, a railway superintendent and the Minster sacristan Albert Gibbs.

In 1911 writer and sociologist Benjamin Seebohm Rowntree enrolled children Mary and Philip at the College.

The oldest former pupil is Phyllis Chappell (née Brown) who attended the school from 1910 until 1917.

Mrs Chappell, now 97, lives at Georgian House, Kirkbymoorside.

York College For Girls pupils and staff, 1908.

She was confirmed at York Minster by the Bishop of Beverley, and moved to Bootham Crescent when she was a child.

"There was an orchard at the other side of the road and the cricket field was quite near," she said. "Later it was turned into a football field."

Mrs Chappell still has fond memories of her schooldays, when making camisoles and petticoats was part of the curriculum. Other lessons included French, Latin and Mathematics.

"We used to play netball in the garden," she added.

Mrs Chappell was one of the first prizewinners and in 1912 she received both an award for Religious Knowledge and the form prize. In 1916/17 she was head girl.

Another story of life at the college was told with exceptional insight by Margaret Mann Phillips, who enrolled in 1919. She died before seeing her book about her time at the college, Willingly To School, published in 1987.

Mrs Phillips, the daughter of the Reverend Francis Mann, rector of St Margaret's, Walmgate, was the first pupil of the college to go to Oxford in 1924.

She went on to enjoy a flourishing academic career, all built on her time at the Petergate school.

In her book, she describes the first headteacher meeting her father. "I can see Miss Ellett (a mathematician, known as T-squared) turning round from her desk, iron-grey hair and pince-nez giving her dignity, to face the new parent."

Her journey to school was an adventure in itself. "The way to school was through the centre of the town, a shortish bicycle ride but hampered by a certain amount of traffic congestion.

"The motor car was just taking over from the horse, but there were still many horse drawn cabs and carts in the streets.

"It was possible and pleasant then to be a reckless cyclist. I eventually used to do the journey in five minutes, darting under the outstretched arm of the policeman on point duty when my brakes refused to work...

"On another occasion I skidded on the wet tramlines and went home with a split chin."

Mrs Phillips' joy of learning initially caused her a few problems at the school.

A prefect once told her: "The girls say you are spending too much time on your homework. They say it's unfair. We aren't supposed to spend more than half an hour on each subject."

Later in the book she recalled prize-giving. "It was preceded by the customary display of pupils' talent, and then T-squared, who was a good hand at publicity where her beloved school was concerned, took it into her head to advertise the fact that we learnt Greek.

"More accurately, one pupil was learning Greek; for the little sandy-haired Latin mistress was now engaged in teaching me the rudiments."

Mrs Phillips' evident fondness for the college is shared by so many of its former pupils, including Gilly Sharper.

Mrs Sharper (née Chapman), of Skelton, is now membership secretary of the Old Girls' Association. Her family's connection with the school reads as a school register.

Her aunt Mary Chapman attended in the late 1930s; her three sisters, Jean, Margaret and Susan all enrolled before her, and she herself left the school in 1964.

Two cousins, Judith Chapman and Susan Fox went there in the 1960s and early 1970s, and another cousin Emma Fox was a pupil at the school when the closure was announced.

Mrs Sharper and her sisters were there when Helena Randall was headmistress.

"She was strict," Mrs Sharper recalled, "but she knew what she wanted.

"When she took the school over it was in a run-down state. She got the new building in the late 1950s which included the new science block and library."

She added: "It was a small school. There were only 11 of us in my class.

"It was a friendly school, too – that's what they will all say."

Training the future captains of industry

IN 1946, the skills of the construction worker were never in more demand. Britain was rebuilding its bomb-shattered cities and its hopes for the future. And the trainee builders of York were making an historic move to a greenfield site just off Tadcaster Road.

Discovering the delights of the theodolite at 'The Tech' in the late 40s.

Before 1946, training had been given at a variety of colleges, most notably at what is now Silks nightclub in Clifford Street. But in September that year, school leavers wanting to learn the trade were the first students of what became the York College of Art and Technology, latterly the York College of Further and Higher Education.

What is now a sprawling, purpose-built campus started off as little more than a barely converted stable block and some Nissen huts.

Some of the teaching took place in Ashfield House, where the senior management of the college work today. The refurbished stables now house the Students' Union.

In those days, potential students would sit an examination at 15, shortly before they left school, in their preferred trade – commerce, engineering or building.

Those who were successful in the latter category began a junior builder's course before becoming an apprentice. There was little money in it during the 1940s – youngsters were paid 9s 6d, or 47.5p a week which worked out at about one pence an hour.

A few years after moving to Tadcaster Road, the construction department of the new college linked up with the York Guild of Building, a relationship which is still going strong today.

The guild has always supported the college's work, awarding its silver medal to the most outstanding student.

Noel Shouksmith, now the curriculum leader at the department, trained at the college – he was a junior builder in 1959 –and returned to become a lecturer after many years in the industry.

In 1970, the college began to break down the sex barrier in what had been an entirely male-dominated industry when Denise Wheatley – now Denise Rowntree – became the first woman in the country to gain a construction technician's certificate. Mrs Rowntree's daughter Emma has followed in her footsteps by taking a similar construction course.

Many senior figures in construction in North Yorkshire were trained at the college and so it has created a strong bond among the building community.

Mr Shouksmith said: "Families tend to work in the industry all their lives and people stay around York because it's such a nice environment.

"In the big cities, there's more turnover. You don't get that same feeling.

"The employer links we have are tremendous. The people who have come through the college who now run their own firms, when they take somebody on, the first thing they do is send them to the Tech to train."

Construction is a notoriously fickle industry, being the first to feel the effects when Britain's economy slumps. "It suffered particularly during the recession," Mr Shouksmith recalled. But the York college is the main training centre for the whole county which has ensured it has always thrived.

The basic skills being taught today are the same as they were when the move was first made to Tadcaster Road 50 years ago. There have been changes in the way students learn their craft, however.

"The way it is taught has changed. It's much more intensive."

Still going strong after 450 years

HANGING above the busy dining hall in what appears to be a typically modern York comprehensive is a set of children's paintings showing some very old faces. For most schools this artwork would perhaps just be the result of a GCSE history project – as distant from teenagers' everyday life as the Magna Carta or 1066.

But for the 450-odd youngsters at Archbishop Holgate's secondary school in Hull Road they serve as a vivid reminder of a continuous school history which goes back about as many years as there are pupils.

Claims to be the oldest anything in a city as ancient as York can get a bit problematic. But headmaster John Harris seems sure of his facts.

"We were the first school in York to be founded," he insists, pointing to surviving copies of the 1546 foundation deed for proof.

This may come as a surprise to York's famous public school St Peter's - which claims roots back to 627AD - but Mr Harris says both schools could trace some sort of ancestry back to that date which was when the Minster was built and cathedral schools are assumed to have started. He argues St Peter's actually received its official foundation 12 years after Archbishop Holgate's in 1558.

Part of the first dining room panel is a picture of the founder Archbishop Robert Holgate, who Mr Harris describes as a sort of Michael Heseltine-type figure – second only to the Henry VIII in terms of power and often standing in for the king in the North of England.

He started the original school in a small building in Ogleforth.

Tucked in behind the Minster in what is today one of York's prettiest streets, the school taught lessons mostly in Latin grammar and composition, with some Greek for the bright boys and maybe even some Hebrew.

Day began and ended with prayers, and on Sundays and Holy Days everyone had to attend worship in the Minster or Holy Trinity in Goodramgate.

The old school house was pulled down in 1667 and replaced with a new one on the same site.

Archbishop Holgate's school in the 1920s - the art room (above) and the ivy-covered classrooms (right). The school, founded in 1546, occupied the site from 1845 to 1963, before moving to a new site on the edge of town.

Despite a few rough patches in the early 19th century when numbers dropped, the school bounced back in 1845 when it moved to the buildings today used by the University College of Ripon and York St John in Lord Mayor's Walk.

Sited next to the teaching training school which was later to become the university college, Archbishop Holgate's blossomed – providing up-to-date teaching in chemistry and engineering as well as traditional subjects.

It aimed at helping boys from farming and trading families to prepare for similar work when they left school at 15, and continued providing

affordable education for the city until well into the 20th century.

Alan Walker was a pupil during the Second World War who later came back to teach until 1992 and recalls the old site well during the wartime years.

"I remember registration where timing depended on whether the 'all-clear' sounded before or after midnight," he said.

The school grew cramped as numbers swelled and in 1961 Harold Macmillan's Britain was busy bringing the country's schools up to date, and York's planners embarked on an ambitious vision for the city's education.

At the same time the University of York was being planned on its massive Heslington campus, a huge patch of farmland bordering it was bought for Archbishop Holgate's 400-year-old grammar school, which eventually moved in in 1963, although the some of the old buildings at Lord Mayor's Walk and the playing fields off Wigginton Road (now the site of York District Hospital) continued to be used for another couple of years.

Former pupil Christopher Brownbridge remembers the move vividly.

"I was sixteen and had just finished doing my O-levels in the Brook Street gym," he said.

"Since I had time on my hands I volunteered to help in moving books and equipment to the new site and spent most of my time in Hull Road unpacking.

"The things which caught my attention first were such things as the push down taps in the toilets, the first I had seen.

"There was the immediate feeling of light and space, not only because of the glass and concrete style of what passed as architecture in the sixties but also because the school was set on top of a hill with the open spaces of playing fields surrounding it."

Not everything went smoothly though. Pupil Ian Melia describes the pitfalls of their new green field home.

"The site was open and superbly placed on top of the glacial moraine with fine views over the Vale of York," he recalls.

"But the beautifully manicured playing fields were littered with stones from the glacial debris. For the first few weeks games were not played but stones were gathered and dropped in buckets."

The last big change came in 1985 when Archbishop Holgate's joined other secondary schools in the city and became a co-educational comprehensive school for pupils aged 11 to 16.

Today the school enjoys better equipment in better furnished rooms than it has ever had before. But that weight of history continues to strengthen its future. Recent bequests have enabled the school to build a modern computer suite and well-equipped new library.

Current pupil Gary Woolway probably sums up the attitude of schoolboys down the ages. "If we could come a bit later in the morning, and finish a bit earlier in the afternoon, things would be just about perfect," he said.

Educating the children of the poor

AMONG the records stored at the Borthwick Institute, Peasholme Green, York, are the archives of the Blue Coat School for boys. There could be no more appropriate place for them, as the school was established in the same building, the medieval St Anthony's Hall, back in 1705.

Retired management consultant and local historian Bill Taylor, of Bishopthorpe, made extensive used of the archives held at Borthwick while researching his excellent book Blue Coat: Grey Coat.

This history, which has just been published, traces the Blue and Grey Coat Schools and the St Stephen's Home of York through from their eighteenth century origins to the 1980s.

It was York Corporation that founded the residential Blue Coat School for boys on Thursday June 14, 1705. This event, Mr Taylor writes, "was probably the most important event in the eighteenth century in the field of education in the City".

It was followed five months later by the opening of the Grey Coat School for girls in premises at the bottom of Marygate.

The schools were established as a reaction to the Charity School movement which had been sweeping the country. Before this time, children from poor families simply were not offered any education.

The impetus came from the Church, which wanted to teach children reading, writing, moral discipline and the scriptures.

By giving poor children the skills for menial work, it was also hoped to save them from vagrancy.

Locally, the movement found support from the Archbishop of York, Dr John Sharp, and the Lord Mayor Charles Redman.

Children could only gain admission through a quarterly ballot of supporters of the school. Each subscriber was initially allowed one vote per boy candidate and one per girl, although this later varied according to the size of the voter's donation.

The name of the Blue Coat School for Boys in York can be traced back to the long blue coats worn by pupils at Christ's Hospital School in London. For more than 100 years, industrial training took precedence over academic and moral education at the Blue Coat school. This helped both to prepare the boys for work and to cover the institution's running costs.

"On leaving the school," Mr Taylor writes, "the boys were fitted out with a suit of clothes and given a Bible and a Book of Common Prayer.

"Each boy received continuing assistance from the school throughout his subsequent period of servitude, which was completed successfully by about half of those bound apprentice."

Living conditions for the boys in the eighteenth century were spartan. There were few washing facilities and it was only in 1780 that a privy was installed.

In the 1820s, discipline at the school broke down with bullying and stealing becoming rife. Boys even sang indecent songs when a mistress was put in charge, and the reputation of the institution sank.

The arrival of the progressive headmaster Edward Robinson in 1863 marked the start of a much better era for the Blue Coat School.

He improved sanitary conditions for the boys and encouraged promising scholars to become pupil teachers. Soon teaching standards had increased enough for students to sit public exams.

In the first half of the 20th century, the school flourished. During the Great War, the school premises suffered slight damage during an air raid by a German Zeppelin airship when a bomb fell on Aldwark, opposite the hall. Fortunately there were no casualties amongst staff or students.

Incendiary bombs also fell on the school in the Second World War and pupils helped to put out a fire in the stable block.

It was not war, therefore, but the 1944 Education Act which finished off the Blue Coat School.

"The school was refused categorisation as a primary, secondary or boarding school and its main purpose as an educational establishment was at an end," Mr Taylor records.

It closed in 1947.

The Grey Coat School for girls, which may have derived its name from the Gray Coat Hospital in Westminster, was initially funded by subscription in the same manner as the boys' school.

It was designed to offer a wholesome and pious education for pupils, who were mostly bound for domestic service when they left.

In the first half of the 1700s, standards were low as the school was sub-contracted to a master and mistress. This allowed them to abuse the system by skimping on meals and using the children as slave labour.

Things improved substantially during the industrial revolution, and in Victorian times the emphasis was on turning out girls with refined values.

In 1900, the curriculum included Bible teachings, cookery, history and geography. By 1905, both schools were celebrating their 200th anniversary and a large reunion of old scholars took place.

Eventually, in 1969, The Grey Coat Home, as it then was, merged with St Stephen's Home. This closed in 1983 - bringing to an end a story begun more than 270 years earlier.

School days spent in the fresh air....

AS every mother knows, fresh air is good for children. It is a principle that was maximised in York for many years, with the city's open air school. The idea was first suggested by Alderman Todd in 1910. At this time, childhood diseases in York were rife. Tuberculosis was a killer, and other illnesses spread quickly in areas of poor, cramped housing such as Hungate, Walmgate and Layerthorpe.

By separating what were termed 'delicate' children from these surroundings and allowing them the benefit of clean air, they stood a greater chance of recovery. It also gave the sick pupils a chance to build up a greater resistance to disease.

The first open air school began in the back garden of the York Tuberculosis Dispensary at number 11 Castlegate.

Initially, 13 children were enrolled. A regime of outdoor lessons, physical exercise and sleep was designed to combat 'consumption'.

The Castlegate arrangement was only meant to be temporary but the First World War intervened.

In the headteacher's log, Miss Ruth Atkin recorded the school's life in those dangerous days.

"29.11.1916. Last night the city was again visited by Zeppelins. Today only 10 of the children attended and these all looked ill, some would have been much better in bed.

"1.12.1916. Before war broke out it was no uncommon thing to find as many as 14 children sleeping soundly. Now only five or six, and these the youngest, really sleep.

"The greater number are watching the sky, and fidgeting the greater part of the time."

So it was not until 1920 that the school moved to more suitable premises.

Fulford Open Air School consisted of a long wooden hut set in 4½ acres, purchased from the Army for about £400, on the site where Fulford Cross School is today. This was to be its home for 40 years.

One of the many pupils who felt the benefit was Brian Sanctuary. Mr Sanctuary recently returned to York to retire after 50 years away, and he is researching a history of the school.

He was previously a pupil at Bilton Street School before being referred by the York Education Board and a medical officer to Fulford.

The average length of stay for children at the open air school was between 12 and 18 months, which was usually enough for their good health

Open air lessons were the order of the day at York Outdoor School in the 1930s.

to be restored. They then went back to their old school.

Mr Sanctuary, however, remained an open air pupil from 1933 to 1938.

"I was there for five years because I was a puny little thing, a 'delicate' little child," he said.

He grew up to be a strapping 6ft tall and served as an infantryman for five years in the British Army - so he could be considered to be a walking advert for the school's methods.

Mr Sanctuary recalled how the front of the Fulford building was fitted with large doors which were flung open to allow as much fresh air as possible into the classrooms.

"In summer, we would pick up our desks and troop out onto the lawns for our lessons.

"The emphasis was always on cleanliness, rhythmic exercises, proper breathing, remedial therapy and a healthy outdoor life."

The exercises helped children recover from such problems as curvature of the spine and rickets.

An important part of the daily routine was the hour after lunch put aside for pupils to sleep in the open air. Outdoor napping went on throughout the year, even in the snow.

"It was a habit that died hard. I still indulge in a snooze after lunch and did so whenever possible during my working life."

Mr Sanctuary believes the teachers "were some of the most dedicated to their task of any in York schools.

"By the 1930s, about 120 children attended the school, and they were regarded by the teachers as their 'family'."

He described Miss Dora Appleby, headmistress for more than a quarter of a century, as "firm but fair, and a real alternative mother to us all", adding that her successor Margaret Hinchcliffe was equally dedicated.

Teacher George Teasdale gave 37 years service to the school and was affectionately nicknamed Uncle Teaze.

In its earliest days, Fulford Open Air School concentrated on exercise and rehabilitation, possibly to the detriment of academic lessons.

"One old boy was heard to say that he knew a lot about raffia work, but not a lot about geography," said Mr Sanctuary.

But the teaching had improved by his day. And throughout its history, the school aided children back to health.

"For many children, it changed their lives.

"Some children had received conventional medical attention for some time.

"After a few months at Fulford Open Air School, they were more or less recovered."

In 1961, the school moved to Beckfield in Acomb. (The old wooden school burned down in four years later.)

Today it is known as Northfield Special School. Mr Sanctuary said: "The present headteacher, Bill Ford, keeps alight the torch which was lit 85 years ago in Castlegate."

Night and day at York Outdoor School. Sleeping under the stars (above) was good for your health, as was PE (below), although those skinny young bodies would have cause alarm nowadays among social workers.

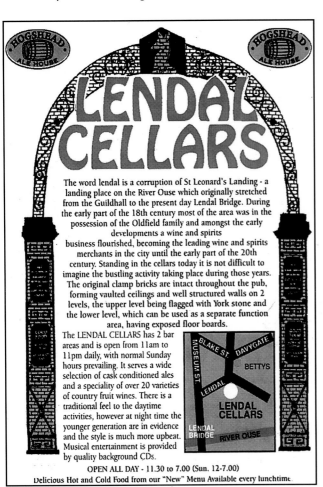

Annie Wilkins' first home: the barge Mary, which plied its trade up and down the River Ouse.

Life on the open road - and on the river!

LITTLE James Henry Whitton didn't like his stepmother. So when he was eight he ran away to live with his uncle in St Margaret's Place, Walmgate, York. That move was to decide the course of the rest of his life. His Uncle Tom ran a boat on the River Ouse and James began to help out.

He took to river life immediately. A few years later, he bought the vessel Mary, and it was launched on July 13, 1910.

In the photograph above, Mr Whitton is seen on the left, at the bow of the barge. His wife, Ruth and other members of the family are in a group at the stern.

Huddled in Mrs Whitton's arms is their daughter, 18-month-old Annie. Now approaching 90, Annie Wilkins lives in Acomb, York. But for the first years of her life, home was the barge Mary.

A door at the bulkhead led down into the cabin via a ladder. Mrs Wilkins said: "My sister, Winnie and I slept in what I called a cupboard, but it was a proper sleeping place".

The family, along with Mr Whitton's workmate, who also lived on board, were kept warm in the winter thanks to a fireplace, which Mrs Whitton also utilised to cook nourishing meals.

York has probably always had transport problems. Its narrow medieval streets soon clog with pedestrians and even horses and carts caused tail-backs. Over the years various remedies have been tried - trams, now being mentioned again as a solution to the city's traffic problems, were seen as the best solution for a long time, and before that the River Ouse was the main highway, taking away the city's exports and bringing most of the city's needs. In this chapter, we discover the delights - and drawbacks - of open-topped trams, the intricacies of a railway system run without the help of modern electronic gadgets and the pioneering joys of the early days of motoring.

Father's pride and joy....

HERE are some friends who knew how to travel in style.

This beautiful car is a 1906 Alldays and Onions model with a 10hp twin cam engine. No doubt it provoked both startled and admiring looks when it was zipping through the North Yorkshire countryside.

With our roads becoming ever more congested, it is difficult to imagine a time when horse-drawn carriages were the main alternative to Shank's pony. But in the first quarter of this century, motorised transport was rare indeed: so this family outing was a definite treat.

The photograph belongs to Joyce Craven of York and features her parents.

Her father James Henry Cave looks resplendent in a bowler hat and her mother Rachel, sits on the right. In the middle is a family friend, Mrs Bramley, with her young son.

Mrs Craven will never forget becoming an early road accident victim as a child - although luckily she wasn't badly hurt.

"I remember I went through the windscreen," she said. "The brakes didn't work - it was at a railway crossing.

"I had been sitting down on a little stool. They wanted to take me to hospital but I wouldn't go."

Brakes or no brakes, such a car is quite rightly a classic and considered very collectable today. Comparing it to the bland, shoe-boxes on wheels that most of us drive around now, the style and design of this motor car is bound to keep it in demand.

Mrs Craven thinks her father bought the Alldays and Onions car for the princely sum of £2. If she still had it in her possession and in good condition, it is safe to say it would be worth considerably more today.

She has a recent newspaper cutting showing the same model being sold for a staggering £11,730: it could even be the one in this picture, but there seems no way to find out.

There was always a cargo waiting to be delivered by the Mary. Cocoa beans were taken to Rowntrees. Coal from the Selby mines was transported to Rymers yard on Monk Bridge, Blundy Clark's yard at Peasholme Bridge and the gas company in York. Grain was taken to many destinations.

"I dropped my dolly into the grain and it sunk right down into the bottom," Mrs Wilkins recalled.

It was an unusual childhood, but she loved it. "If we laid anywhere for a day, we were supposed to go to school - but we didn't.

"We didn't like school very much. My mum taught us to read and write, and our times tables. We were very happy."

The barge had a mast and two sails, but no engine. When she was ready to leave what the family called their 'home' berth, Castle Mills basin in York, she usually started her journey pulled along by a tug. A horse on the tow-path provided the power for journeys such as that along Selby Canal.

When the First World War broke out, Mrs Wilkins remembers watching the German Zeppelins overhead.

"People used to dash down to the boats and the river for safety", she said.

Houses and factories were the targets for the bombs.

One Christmas, when the family was at Heworth, someone let the boat loose from its mooring at Rymers yard. Her father had to use the horse to retrieve it after it drifted down the River Foss.

Mrs Wilkins still misses life on the river. "It was lovely. We used to get away. And when we got back to York and laid up in Castle Mills basin my dad always took us to Fishergate Picture Palace.

"There were lots of boats. There were a lot of people we know who had children on board. Everything was home-cooked by my mum. She was lovely and my father was an angel. It was fun."

Her father eventually took over responsibility for running the lock at Ferrybridge. Mrs Wilkins got her first job when she was 14 with Poulson's Pottery, Ferrybridge.

"I worked there until the General Strike in 1926. They ran out of coal - they couldn't get any more.

"Then they closed down and I had to go back to York."

End of the long line from London....

IN 1996, a £450,000 project reclaimed 700-metres of the Ripon Canal and its terminal basin, re-establishing the most northerly point on the country's connected waterway network. The scheme made it possible to travel from London to Ripon

The end of the line: Ripon Canal Basin at the end of the last century, when it was possible to travel all the way to London by boat.

by boat for the first time since 1935. But the canal goes back much further – to the 18th century in fact.

Plans to extend navigation on the River Ouse to Ripon by means of work to the River Ure and a two-and-a-quarter mile canal were realised by an Act of Parliament in 1767.

It was a huge boost to the city, as it would give access by water not only to York, but to the Humber and the port of Hull.

Previously, the only method of transporting goods was the poor old pack horse.

A survey was carried out and estimates prepared under the supervision of the renowned engineer John Smeaton, the designer of the third Eddystone Lighthouse.

His ambitious £7,500 plan included five locks and proposed the construction of one of the first cast iron bridges in the country, to carry the Great North Road over the Milby Cut at Boroughbridge (that was replaced by the present roundabout in 1946).

John Smith, a Doncaster engineer, oversaw the work, which was completed in 1770. By that time, the canal scheme was in debt to the tune of £11,450 and the Ripon Canal Company was sold to the Ure Navigation Company.

Vessels of up to 30 tons brought coal and other products to Ripon and returned with cargoes of butter, cheese and lead. New warehouses and wharves were built at the canal basin to handle the trade.

The canal warehouse and manager's house still remain today.

The decline of commercial trade on the canal was brought about by the development of Britain's railway network. Even the growing use by pleasure craft could not prevent the dereliction and demise of the upper stretch of the canal.

Although the navigation profited from carrying materials to build the Great North of England Railway (opened between York and Darlington in 1841), the coming of the Leeds and Thirsk Railway provided a faster means of transporting goods to and from Ripon.

In 1846 the Ure Navigation Company was bought by the Leeds and Thirsk Railway. Despite the company's obligation to keep the navigation open and in good repair, by 1857 it was suffering from neglect.

The canal enjoyed commercial use up until the 1970s, but pleasure craft represented the only growth in traffic from the 1930s. The Ripon Motor Boat club was formed and remains at Littlethorpe Marina.

By 1935 the upper canal was unnavigable and in the mid-1950s construction of an extension to Littlethorpe Road severed the last 700 metres of the canal from the rest of the navigation. The locks at Rhodes Field and Bells Furrow were blown up by the Ripon Corporation because it was feared they would attract vandals.

Restoration begin in 1983 thanks to the enthusiastic efforts of the Ripon Canal Society. British Waterways, the body which looks after the canal, estimates the economic benefits from its reopening through boat trips, angling and tourism would total more than £350,000. It seems like the canal is to enjoy a second golden age.

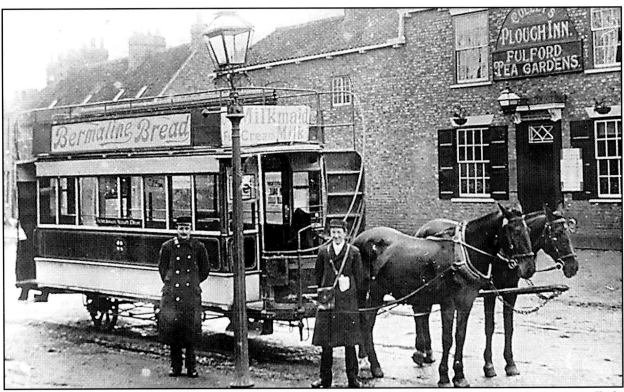

The early days: This 1905 picture of the Fulford tram outside the Plough Inn demonstrates how little the York suburb has changed - except for the traffic. For this quiet street is Main Street, now a bustling thoroughfare at virtually any hour of the day.

One of the first electric trams in York crosses Lendal Bridge. Electric trams replaced the horse drawn version in 1910 and this picture probably dates from the the First World War. Note the absence of any other motorised transport. The horse - and the bicycle - still provided much of the city's transport.

At the mercy of the weather....

TRAFFIC congestion can bring York and cities around the world to a standstill. After originally confining them to the dustbin on history, trams are now being considered by many city authorities as a way to free their streets from the scourge of the car.

The EuroTram, which ferries people across Strasbourg every few minutes, is a lasting legacy to the skills of the York ABB workforce who built it.

This is the futuristic face of a transport system which made its first, horse-drawn appearance, in York in the late 19th century.

Electric trams took over and were an integral part of York for years, before their final demise in 1935.

Evening Press reader Kathleen Clifford of Nunthorpe Crescent, York, has mixed memories of this short-lived form of transport. Here are her recollections of travelling by tram ...

"We must have been a hardy lot in days of yore! I don't mean centuries ago, I mean in my childhood years - the 1920s and 30s.

"We stood in the snow and rain, waiting for the tram. If we were lucky, we managed to squeeze inside; if downstairs was full, we were told curtly by the conductor that it was 'upstairs only'.

"Up there, there was no roof and no glass round the sides. We were prevented from falling into the street by a rail about waist high. In the centre of the upper deck was a metal stanchion which supported the electric trolley.

"This connected the live wire overhead with the inner-workings below - a process which I could never understand and never found anyone who could explain it to me. The seats held two passengers and were composed of narrow slats which must have left a long-lasting impression on one's nether anatomy.

"The back of the seats were slats also, and these could be moved to and fro so that at journey's end, they were pushed to the opposite side of the seats, thus enabling passengers to face the way they were going.

"A journey up there in inclement weather had to be experienced to be appreciated. Depending on the direction of the wind (and it always seemed to be blowing!) we were coated with snow on our fronts or our backs.

"But when it was raining, we were soaked through in any case.

"Both ends of the tram were alike. The driver stood in front of the glassless window and twirled two levers.

"Separating him from the passengers were two sliding doors. When the terminus was reached, he slid these open, passed down the aisle and stationed himself at the other end.

"The conductor's duties consisted of punching and distributing tickets as he walked between the passengers. Tickets were different colours for the different stages - orange, green, purple, blue, red and white. You got a 'transfer' if you wished to change trams during your journey.

"Below stairs there was the added refinement of glass windows and, of course, a ceiling but the journey was quite hazardous. The tram rocked violently at times, particularly as it negotiated the 'points' and was so noisy that conversation was almost impossible.

"Passengers sat facing one another on the equivalent of elongated slatted park benches. If it was standing room only we had to be quick and grab one of the strap handles hanging from the ceiling or we were catapulted down the aisle ending up with a crash against the driver's double doors.

"In the summer, though, things were different. On a sunny evening we would board the tram at Knavesmire terminus for a ride on the top storey to Fulford.

"We'd leave the cricketers and the children to play on Knavesmire and off we'd go. It was exciting to sit high above the streets, with the chestnut blossom almost touching our heads.

"We could see into the rooms above the familiar shops below; there were pleasure boats chugging down the Ouse leaving V-shapes in their wakes.

"The swallows curved through the evening sky; we could look down into people's gardens where they were working or sitting or chatting over the fence.

"When we arrived at the terminus up we got, changed sides and the seat backs and off we went again, seeing the other side of the road from this moving vantage point.

"Eventually we returned to Knavesmire feeling we'd had an adventure. The cricketers were still making their runs, the children still laughing and playing in the sunshine."

The old and the new: A horse-drawn tram (above) attempts the steep climb up Micklegate hill. Presumably the horse being walked alongside was a spare should the slope prove too much. Pictured below is a 'new-fangled' electric tram on the Nessgate-Fulford run - and jam-packed!

Trams give way to the motor bus....

YORK'S history as a transport city is well chronicled. The number of each locomotive that regularly passed through York station and the factories that manufactured every tram and omnibus are on record. But the story of those who worked in the industry is less well know.

One man who is trying to change that is Noel Smith, a Rider York bus inspector in York. Mr

Retired public transport staff before a day out - by bus, naturally - in the 1950s. Former tram driver Tom Lund is pictured second from the left on the front row.

Smith, who has worked in public transport for more than 30 years, is writing a book about the people whose lives have been devoted to keep the city moving.

Tram driver Tom Lund is one of his subjects, and his working days make for fascinating reading. Much of the information and pictures were provided by Tom's daughter, Joan Merryweather, of Shipton Street, York.

Shortly after his birth in 1890, Tom's family moved to Lowther Street, York. He went to Park Grove School and for the next 10 years had a variety of jobs. He started at Anderson's Tailors in Coney Street – his mother was a dressmaker – and later worked as a footman at Bishopthorpe Palace.

It was in 1912 that Tom started on the trams, a very sought after job.

Two years later he joined the Royal Artillery at the start of the First World War. He was later awarded the Military Medal for charging a German gun emplacement.

Tom had married during leave in 1916 and lived with his wife in Nunnery Lane, York. After the war, he was employed again by the Electric Lighting and Tramway Department, as a motorman – the official title given to tram drivers.

His bravery, demonstrated during the war, was in evidence again by a dramatic incident in 1920. Tom was driving over Skeldergate Bridge when he spotted a child in the River Ouse, clearly in difficulty.

He stopped the tram and dived into the river, pulling the child to safety. A citation from the city council, dated May 7, 1920, commended his courage and acknowledged the members' decision to apply for him to receive a Certification from the York Swimming Club & Humane Society.

Tom also received £5 from the child's parents, which was a massive reward at the time - equivalent to two weeks' wages.

On another occasion, a sack of coal fell from a horse-drawn cart in front of his tram. Tom stopped, heaved the sack on to the car and later delivered it to the home address. This was a particularly honest gesture as it happened in 1926, the year of the General Strike.

Tom drove three different forms of transport – the trams, trolley buses and petrol buses with solid wheels. In 1934, West Yorkshire Road Car bought the operation out from the York Corporation.

He was then working in the Barbican Road depot and did local work as well as long distance trips.

As a captain in the Home Guard during the Second World War, Tom travelled to Hull on many a night to help out: the city was heavily bombed.

On his retirement in 1955, Tom worked part-time at the barracks in Fulford Road and worked there for years. He died in 1974 at the age of 84.

End of an era for the railways....

WHEN George VI was crowned king at Westminster Abbey on May 12, 1937, a few hundred miles up the road another ceremony was taking place. This was not quite as grand, but had far-reaching consequences for travellers in North Yorkshire.

It was the opening of the newly dualled section of the A64 between York and Malton. Even back then, traffic heading to the coast was building up, and North Riding County Council chose to upgrade the road.

This change had a knock-on effect for the railways. At Barton Hill there were two level crossings on the York to Scarborough line, one over the A64 and the other over the road to Barton-le-Willows.

There was a signalbox at each crossing, but the decision to dual the road meant the end to the one next to the A64.

In his book A History of the York-Scarborough Railway, Bill Fawcett writes about the Barton village station. It "was built at the Barton crossing but replaced almost immediately by one at the turnpike, and by March 1850 the York and North Midland Railway Company was seeking to let the former station house.

"It is very similar to Haxby and was eventually converted into two dwellings for signalmen."

One of those signalmen is James Shipley, who moved to the converted station with his wife Alice in 1951. They are still there today, next to the 1936-built signal box manned by his successors.

Mr Shipley, worked on the railways at Pocklington and Whitby before his first stint at Barton Hill in 1937.

Later that same year he worked at Coxwold where he became a fully fledged signalman and, more importantly, met Alice.

From 1942-1951, he was based at Holtby on the Hull line. Strict regulations governing the lights on the train were introduced during the war.

In the terrible winter of 1947, Mr Shipley and a track engineer worked almost non-stop to keep their stretch of line clear of snow and help to ensure that services continued running.

There were not many regular train services from York to Scarborough in those days. A hand-written timetable from 1950 showed that the first service left York at 4.30am and the last at

Locomotive Blue Peter pulls out of York Station for its regular job of hauling The Scarborough Flyer.

8pm. The same number came the other way.

But with the huge popularity of the East Coast as a holiday resort, extra services in summer increased Mr Shipley's workload considerably.

On one occasion he remembers being transferred to Haxby and dealing with 80 trains in one shift.

"We were rushing about like scalded cats at one time," he said.

Among the great steam locomotives he would see safely along the York-Scarborough line were the Scarborough Flyer and the Blue Peter.

Mr Shipley shared two shifts with a colleague at Barton Hill: 4.25am to 12.25pm, and 12.25pm to 9pm.

Until 1965, when the station was closed, there was also a station master who worked office hours. In Mr Shipley's days it was Harry Burrill.

"In my day, if you kept your nose clean, it was a job for life," explained Mr Shipley. "There's no such thing these days.

"Wages were poor. The basic pay was very poor, but here there was a lot of overtime."

Inside the Barton Hill box were 16 levers operating the signals and points as well as a wheel which operated the gate shutting off the level crossing. Another duty would include loading the trains with parcels and other goods.

For many years, signalmen kept a record of the day's incidents in an Occurrence Book, and it is here where a note was made of the opening of the A64 dual carriageway on the day of George VI's coronation.

Mr Shipley said there were never problems with the leaves on the line back then - but sheep on the line - wandering from Strensall Common - did hold up the steam trains.

One exciting episode that came too late to be recorded in an Occurrence Book was instead reported in the Sunday People newspaper.

"One hundred passengers jumped for their lives after an express train caught fire," the edition from May 17, 1969 stated.

The Scarborough to Leeds service had burst into flames at Barton Hill. Scarborough passenger Douglas Pepper spotted smoke.

"We're in a diesel," he told his wife. "There shouldn't be any smoke!"

Thanks to his quick-thinking, no-one was hurt.

Mr Shipley retired in 1980 after 45 years service. Amongst his near neighbours are his daughter and grand-daughter.

He still sees the trains rush by - but the sprinter trains, however efficient, just don't hold the same romance as those wonderful old steam engines.

Paying the price of crossing the River Ouse....

WHEN Norman Henderson bought the Evening Press book York Then And Now 2, the picture of Skeldergate Bridge in 1893 held a special fascination for him.

Mr Henderson's grandfather, William, was tollmaster at the bridge – and at Lendal Bridge before tolls were abolished there on August 7, 1894.

William Henderson's engineering background with the North Eastern Railway had secured him the post at Skeldergate Bridge. It meant he would have no trouble operating the lifting machinery which allowed cargo boats to pass along the river.

In his obituary, published the day after his death in the York Herald of January 20, 1910, it said: "When Mr Henderson held the Skeldergate Bridge lease, there was no necessity for the corporation to appoint an engineer to cater for the opening and shutting of the bridge for the passage of large vessels, his knowledge of the profession enabling him to do all that."

An engineering report to York Corporation on Skeldergate Bridge in February 1882, by Mr G Page, revealed that the bridge had cost more than anticipated to build – rather like every project of a similar scale since.

It broke its budget because of problems with flooding, the "characters of the foundations" and the hydraulic equipment.

The lifting machinery was "placed in a watertight cellar in an abutment below the bridge", the report went on.

And there was more to the toll house than might have been expected. It was a "dwelling house, with the ground floor about one foot above the flood level, comprising kitchen, scullery, larder, bedroom, large cellar, coal cellar under stairs."

A document dating from January 1893 shows that Mr Henderson paid £1,305 to York Corporation for a three-year lease to operate the tolls.

The York (Skeldergate Bridge) Improvement Act 1875 set the tolls, although the bridge did not open to pedestrians or traffic until 1881.

This is a very thorough document. It states that a "sum not exceeding" two old pence would be paid "for every horse or beast of draught drawing any coach, omnibus, chariot, Landau, Britzska, Brougham, sociable, Berlin, Victoria chaise, curricle, phaeton, gig, cabriolet, dog-cart, whiskey, car, calash, caravan, hearse, or litter-waggon, wain, van, cart, wherry, implement or

Skeldergate Bridge at the end of the last century. The newly-constructed bridge provided a vital link between the north and south banks of the rapidly-expanding city - and a lucrative source of income for the toll master.

other wheeled carriage" to cross the bridge.

Mr Henderson kept a daily tally of his takings in beautiful copperplate handwriting.

These records show that he regularly made £30 a week – a handsome sum which justified the expense of the lease and the rates.

With the profits, he built 20 Cromwell Road, just round the corner from Skeldergate Bridge. William Henderson died little more than a year after his grandson, Norman, was born, and Cromwell Road because Norman's childhood home.

His father, William Woolatt Henderson, was a hairdresser, with a salon initially in Nessgate, then Bridge Street and finally in Micklegate. He was made a freeman of the city, an honour which passed to his son.

Norman lives in Riseborough House, Rawcliffe Lane, York. He spent 36 years as a schoolteacher in the city, retiring as headteacher of Danesmead School in 1970.

Mr Henderson was first appointed a head-teacher in 1939, when he took charge of Scarcroft School.

"War broke out in September 1939, and schools were closed," he remembered.

"It was part-time education for everybody until the air raid shelters were built."

The bombing raid in 1942 destroyed Poppleton Road School. The education authority decided Poppleton students would move to Scarcroft School and Mr Henderson would move his school to an empty wing of Knavesmire School.

But there were no desks or equipment at Knavesmire and Mr Henderson had to scrounge everything from other schools.

Pioneering Don Brown at the controls of a mechanised combine harvester in 1947. Don and his brother Lawrence produced the first self-propelled combine harvester in the country, utilising their Army experience, and revolutionised farming.

Don's bright idea eased farmers' workloads

FARMS today are full of expensive, high tech equipment. So much so that in recent years North Yorkshire farmers have become the targets for commuter criminals. But robbers would have found little equipment worth stealing from farms in the earlier part of this century. Much of the work was done by hand.

That accounts for the amount of interest generated when the late Donald Brown and his brother Lawrence produced the first self-propelled mechanical combine harvester in the country in 1947.

Don had first rented some old farm buildings in Askham Bryan, near York, in the 1940s, where he carried out repairs on agricultural equipment. When Lawrence came out of the Army, he joined his brother's business.

In 1947, the mechanical combine harvester itself was nothing new. But it was a cumbersome,

> **Work never changes. For the vast majority of us, the period between leaving school and taking retirement is filled with many years of work. But some things have changed. Hours are generally shorter, we have more leisure time and working conditions have generally changed for the better.**

horse-drawn machine which was very difficult to manoeuvre.

The Browns adapted a former Army tractor unit and fitted it to the combine, and the country's first self-propelled combine harvester had been invented.

ABOVE: Askham Bryan garage,
built by the Brown brothers in
1960 - the first time the village
had seen petrol pumps.

RIGHT: May Brown racing
her go-kart in the 1960s.

"We never made a fuss about it,"
said Lawrence, who still lives in
Askham Bryan.

The papers did however, and it
made a big splash in the Evening
Press at the time.

They hired out their invention to
local farmers.

"We both went round the farms
cutting the corn," Lawrence recalled.

The service was popular as it was far faster
than any other methods available at that time.
But the machine came to an abrupt end.

Lawrence said: "We never got any further
because it went up in smoke. I went back at
night to remove the battery and I got it trapped."

A spark flew from the battery and set the petrol
and paraffin fuelled machine, as well as a nearby
straw stack, alight.

By the time the fire brigade arrived the mobile
combine was gutted.

An account of these events is found in Askham
Bryan Remembered II, by Mary Carbert.

Despite the setback of the fire, the Browns'
business went from strength to strength. Don
married May and built the Askham Bryan garage
in 1960, installing the first petrol pumps in the
village. Their house was built next door.

Don became the agent for Hillman cars, selling
the famous Imp. He also sold a make of car
imported from Russia called the Moskvitch.

May, of Dringhouses, York, said running the
garage was hard work. She would serve
motorists with petrol – no self service in those
days – which cost just 4s 3d a gallon. In her
spare time, she took part in kart races, winning a
silver cup in 1960.

A policeman's lot was not always a happy one....

CLOSED circuit television cameras
watching York became fully opera-
tional in 1996. They were the latest
addition to a high-tech armoury
deployed in the fight against crime,
which includes quick-cuffs, satellite
tracking and 'stingers' which immobilise stolen
cars.

How baffling it would be to a member of the
very first City of York Police force. That was
established on April 30, 1836, and was so poorly
equipped that every officer signed a petition, sent
to the Watch Committee in 1844, complaining at
long hours, poor pay and insufficient resources to
police a city of 40,000 people.

Before the force was set up, York was 'policed'
by watchmen who patrolled at night. The city

was forced to formalise the arrangement by the Municipal Corporations Act of 1835.

This law required every borough to set up a Watch Committee which would "appoint a sufficient number of day and night constables who shall be sworn in before a Justice having jurisdiction within the Borough".

Minutes of the Watch Committee record that the first "Captain of Patrol and Head Constable" was one Daniel Smith. He would receive 25 shillings per week, with other constables receiving 18s.

All but one of the nine men who made up the first police force were members of the night watch. One watchman had declined to serve in the new constabulary, so another man was appointed in his place.

By August 1836, the force had undergone its first reorganisation. A Metropolitan superintendent who inspected the men, at the request of the Watch Committee, recommended the extension of the force to 20 officers.

That was ignored, probably on cost grounds, but other changes - including the adoption of the Metropolitan dress complete with the lantern, rattle, staff and handcuffs - were introduced by October.

By all accounts, the force was very disorderly. The first arrest of a constable happened within a month of the force being set up. He was later released from jail to continue his duties.

Officers were often found drunk and disorderly on their beat. The punishment was usually either a severe reprimand by the chairman of the Watch Committee or a fine of a day's wages.

The Watch Committee contains many examples of the unprofessional behaviour from the policemen: "PC Corner was reported for having stopped a person named Edward Grimshaw in St Leonard's Place last Sunday morning, who had in his pocket a hen and a rook, and allowing him to escape without giving any alarm...

"PC Corner was severely reprimanded by the committee, and cautioned that he ought to spring his rattle under the circumstances stated."

The first police station was in Silver Street which, according to a Government inspector's report in 1857, was none too pleasant. It condemned the serious overcrowding in the cells and the lack of both heating and sanitation.

"On the occasion of the visit now adverted to, there were no prisoners and evident preparations had been made for inspection by washing and sanding the floors, nevertheless there remained a most offensive odour," the report's author fulminated.

"On a former occasion, however, when a visit had not been anticipated, I not only found the cells occupied, but I found them in a most disgraceful state, the walls and floor of one wet by the admission of rain, and the whole filthy and

The East Yorkshire Yorkshire Constabulary of the last century, equipped with bicycle transport and providing an ambulance service.

ABOVE: No, not Dr Who's tardis, but a police box, once a familiar sight now long disappeared.

BELOW: A collection of York Police Force uniforms through the ages.

indescribably offensive."

The force increased in size with York. In 1886, when the city population numbered 61,000, there were 68 policemen. An additional station had been built in Alma Terrace by this time. Work on the present police station in Fulford Road was completed in 1892.

Writing in Police Box, the magazine of North Yorkshire police, on the occasion of the force's 150th anniversary, Andrew Campbell noted how the First World War had a significant effect on York police practice.

"The manpower was depleted by men joining the Armed Forces; four men were killed in the war and are commemorated on a plaque in the Magistrates' Court.

"The threat of large civilian casualties, through bombing, dominated the work of the force and contingencies were prepared - cellars and other safe places were found and logged.

"In the end, it was a threat that did not materialise until the Second World War some 20 years later."

The city had been divided into 34 beats, but this was slimmed down to 18 with the arrival in 1929 of an early piece of bobby technology, the police box.

"The police box was the base for the beat constable," Mr Campbell wrote. "His work both started and finished there.

"Whereas before the men went back to the station at intervals during the middle of each shift for refreshment, now they ate in the box itself.

"Contact with the officer was via the flashing light on top of the box. Getting anywhere fast was a matter of jumping on a passing tram."

Today, police use helicopters, CCTV and computers to keep up with the criminal. The police force has come a long way since those nine men with their rattles patrolled their beat in 1836.

Upper Poppleton Post Office at the beginning of the century.

Waiting for the mail van....

FOR more than 100 years, the National Federation of Sub-Postmasters has represented local businessmen and women across the country. The trade union was formed on Easter Monday, 1897, by Wakefield sub-postmaster Joseph Ranns.

At that time, post offices had to open for up to 16 hours a day (only 12 hours on Christmas Day!) and there were no breaks for holiday and no sickness pay.

Sub-postmasters had to pay to work for the Post Office, and also had to meet office expenses and the cost of putting up telegraph wires.

Peter Wykes, president of the federation's 102-member York branch, and his wife Maureen have run the sub post-office at Nether Poppleton, near York, since 1992.

The village's post office was once a railway carriage. It was replaced by a cabin-like structure and then by the present, more conventional building.

Local photograph collector Laurie Inman supplied the picture on this page of the old post office at neighbouring Upper Poppleton.

This photograph, dating from early this century, shows three men – one wearing a postman's uniform – standing outside the thatched building. The sign over the door reads "S Standish, Grocer & Provision Dealer, Licensed to Sell Tobacco".

This was the birthplace and childhood home of Dorothy Bramma. Now in her 90s, Dorothy recounted how her mother Miss Maria Standige inherited the business from the aunt who brought her up.

Miss Standige married Samuel Standish, whose name is that on the sign. Mr Standish can be seen in the foreground of the picture with his dog Spot.

"He was up very early delivering the mail," said Mrs Bramma who lives in York.

"On a Sunday Dad used to take the mail down to the end of Station Road in Poppleton on to the York road.

"He would wait for the mail van coming from Boroughbridge. We used to go with him."

Mrs Bramma's mother and father gave up the business when she was seven.

They feared the growing popularity of the telephone might hit business and they went back into farming. The building was demolished some years later.

Bill and Joan Spence, both in their 70s, run the sub post office at Ampleforth College – the only one in Britain to have a school's name as its postmark.

Mr Spence took over as sub-postmaster in 1977 after the death of his wife's mother, Hilda Ludley.

She began running the Ampleforth College post office with her husband William in 1920, only four years after it opened.

Mrs Spence's grandparents, John and Rhoda Ludley, had the post office in Ampleforth village from 1886 to 1939, and her grandmother's uncle, Frank Thompson ran it before that.

Mr Spence said: "My wife really runs the post office, and always has done."

She delivered post around the college and neighbouring properties for about 56 years until last year, taking about three hours on foot to complete the round.

"The postman in 1940 was taken off for the war effort," said Mr Spence. "She took it on temporarily until he came back.

"But he didn't want the job when he came back, so she stayed on and became probably the longest serving postwoman in the country."

Her efforts have been rewarded with a British Empire Medal and the Imperial Service Medal.

The post office, serving the Roman Catholic public school, has a character all of its own.

Mr Spence said: "It quietens down during holiday times, but it's a very busy office during term time.

"We do a completely different trade to a village office. We are dealing mostly with males, most of whom are under 18s."

Mr and Mrs Spence's twin daughters, Geraldine and Judith, enjoy helping out in the post office.

"It's bred in them I suppose," Mr Spence said. "My wife always says that if I pull at her ear, stamps will come out."

William Simpson, butler to York's Lord Mayor, stands proudly below the city's coat of arms.

The unofficial Ambassador....

LOOK at photographs of any royal visit to York over a 40-year period and it is likely that a distinguished figure will be standing discreetly in the background. This is William Simpson, known alternatively as Mr Mansion House and the unofficial Ambassador of York. His official title was butler and attendant to the Lord Mayor.

Mr Simpson celebrated his 90th birthday recently. Most of that long life has been spent in York: he was born near Newcastle but moved to the city when he was four years old.

When he was a young boy, he lived with parents, his three sisters and brother, and his grandparents at their house at 2 Little Shambles.

His grandfather, Mr Storey, had been coachman to the famous Wilberforce family, and was then running his own horse and cab which stood at the Parliament Street rank.

Next door at 3 Little Shambles were the Bumby family, the city's official bill posters until they sold the business to another family called the Sheldons.

The street came off Big Shambles, known today simply as Shambles. Mr Simpson remembers an enclosed yard close by called Gell Garth. Cattle were driven along Carter's Passage to Gell Garth for slaughter: the gullies were sloped so the blood would drain away.

"In Shambles in those days, there were 31 butchers shops," Mr Simpson said. "They used to have big oak tables where they used to put the meat."

He could also name the four public houses on the little street – the Shoulder of Mutton, The Neptune, The Eagle and Child and The Globe.

Nearby, on Jubbergate, there was Webster's tin shop, and on the way to Newgate you could find Muir's shop, which repaired prams and sold bags of coal for one old penny.

"In Colliergate at that time you could go to the soup kitchen and buy a big jug of soup, thick with meat and vegetables, plus bread, for sixpence."

In St Sampson's Square stood the hot potato machine, complete with a box of salt on the side, and the potman who used to bang his china on a tea chest to show how strong it was.

Mr Simpson's father Charles worked at the Army Ordnance Department on Wenlock Terrace, Fulford Road, checking the supplies brought in and out on mule carts.

"When I was in Wenlock Terrace, I saw the first German Zeppelin to come over York. You could see little black figures moving about inside.

"There were crowds of people on the streets. It was really good to watch.

Butler William Simpson polishes a piece of York Mansion House's silver.

"They never thought about anyone dropping bombs. It was just exciting in those days."

After leaving school, he worked as a pantry boy at St John's College. That was where he was introduced to his future wife Nan, later to work with him a cook at the Mansion House.

At the age of 16, he went into private service as a hall boy for Colonel Philip Saltmarsh, at Saltmarsh Hall near Howden. Duties included cleaning the household's shoes. He was paid £2 a month, sending 30 shillings home to his mother.

This began Mr Simpson's long career in service, which saw him work at stately homes throughout the north.

He was following a family tradition. "My mum had been a cook. My grandma and granddad were both in private service. It was thought to be the thing to do in those days."

He climbed the below-stairs career ladder graduating from hall boy to butler.

Working at Harewood House, he attended the late Queen Mary when she came to visit. "She was very, very sweet, was Queen Mary," he smiled.

In 1934, he joined the staff at the Mansion House. Coun Harrowell was Lord Mayor and among the highlights of his first year were the visit of the Australian Prime Minister and the enthronement of the Bishop of Ripon.

Initially he was the assistant butler and the mace bearer, later being promoted to butler and sword bearer.

Service uniform was a smart black jacket and pinstriped trousers; a red coat and chain of office was de rigeur for functions.

For the quarterly assizes, the judges would ceremonially make their way from what is now the Judge's Lodgings Hotel to the Mansion House for breakfast, accompanied by fanfares.

Mr Simpson would take part in the procession, bearing the sword, behind a civic party which included the Lord Mayor, Sheriff and the Chief Constable.

A fanfare heralded the judges' arrival and welcomed them to the city.

They feasted on fish, bacon, eggs, tomatoes, cutlets, and strawberries and cream.

"Now you realise why when the judges sat on the bench, they had their eyes closed sometimes."

In his time in service, he has attended almost every member of the royal family from Queen Mary to the present sovereign. The Queen, as Princess Elizabeth, came to York in 1950, returning only a year after her Coronation.

"It's remarkable," he said. "Whenever you looked after royalty they always remember your name."

Mr Simpson was also at several Buckingham Palace garden parties – where he used to join the footmen for a cup of tea – and has been in official attendance at Sandringham and Kensington Palace.

He attended numerous other VIPs, including six Archbishops of York, Prime Minister Edward Heath and the American Ambassador.

In 1972, Mr Simpson retired, having served 38 Lord Mayors. His skill at his job had led to several appearances on national television and radio, and a lucrative offer of employment in America.

"The old type of British butler is the finest in the world," he says. Judging by his track record at least, you cannot argue with that.

Rowntree Park: a haven of fun for York youngsters for more than 70 years.

The all-seeing Parkie Bell

BETWEEN the wars, children getting up to mischief in Rowntree Park - scrumping apples, chasing the ducks or, heaven forbid, walking on the grass - were usually being watched.

Parkie Bell could see everything that went on from his hut next to the tennis courts. As soon as he spotted any naughtiness he would blow his whistle, shake his walking stick and inform the miscreants in his cockney accent to 'clear orf'.

James Bell was the first attendant at Rowntree Park. He was one of the most well-known and fondly-regarded characters in York, policing the park from its opening in 1921 until his death in 1945.

The Rowntree family offered to create the park as a memorial to their staff who had fallen in the Great War. Joseph Rowntree officially handed over the deeds to the then Lord Mayor, Alderman Edward Walker, in a formal ceremony before the gates were thrown open to the public.

The Yorkshire Evening Press reporter attending the opening was very impressed with the snack bar "where those who wish may obtain hot water free of charge."

Many of the original features of the park have vanished or altered beyond recognition over the years. An aviary housing exotic birds used to be very popular. A small pond decorated with a statue of Eros has long since gone. No-one knows what happened to the statue.

The children's play area boasted wooden-framed swings and a sandy floor to provide a soft

Leisure time might not have been as abundant in earlier years as it is now, but that didn't stop people going out and enjoying themselves. Some of their hobbies and pastimes are still popular, others have disappeared into the realms of history. The pressures of work, war and poverty may have limited free time but what is clear in this chapter is that people were determined to get some fun out of life.

landing. There was also a paddling pool, but youngsters had to look out for blood-sucking red worms that lurked in the water. The sunken rose garden had to be raised after regularly falling victim to floods.

Today, only the base of the bandstand remains, but the full structure hosted regular concerts for many years.

Military bands would perform and Waddington's music company would play gramophone records every Wednesday.

Waitresses, complete with little white aprons and caps, served refreshments from the café.

No-one knows Rowntree Park like Jean Tattersfield, the daughter of Parkie Bell. She was

ABOVE: Master of all he surveys, Parkie Bell keeps watch from his hut in Rowntree Park.

BELOW: Two of the park's attractions - the children's play area, which is still there in an amended form, and the aviaries, which have long since disappeared.

born in the park-keeper's house, as were her brother John and sister Yvonne. Her eldest sister Eileen, who loved the park, died in 1994.

Mrs Tattersfield recalled a childhood in which she imagined their family house was a stately home and the park was its grounds. At that time, there were at least 10 staff tending the gardens and looking after the animals.

A tennis tournament would be held in summer with the Lord Mayor amongst the spectators sitting in a specially constructed stand.

She can remember people skating on the frozen pond in the winter.

"In the morning, they would scrape the ice and then brush it ready for the skating in the afternoon and evening," she said.

"One half was for the skaters and the other half was for children to play on".

The pond is only a couple of feet deep, so there was no danger involved. In fact a group of children were once gathering on the ice for a photograph when it gave way and they fell in.

Any youngsters who got wet or hurt themselves would go to see Mrs Tattersfield's mother Edith at their house in the park and be dried off or bandaged up.

During the war, the Government encouraged a Holidays at Home scheme. Rowntree Park was one of the venues and special events were organised to take people's minds off the hardship.

Donkeys were even brought along to give the children rides. "Some of the ruffians from Clementhorpe got in and tried to let the donkeys out," Mrs Tattersfield recalled. Together with her mother she foiled the raid.

Mrs Tattersfield and her family left the house in Rowntree Park after her father's death in 1945 when she was 17, to allow the new park keeper to move in. She still keeps a close interest in the park today and has wonderful memories of her younger days.

"It was a special childhood," she said. "We had the privilege of being there on the spot to enjoy it all."

Heading for the fairways

FORMAL dress was required for a game of golf earlier in the century.

The women were in bonnets, the men in three piece suits.

Who was actually going to enjoy a round on the links is unclear but two sets of clubs are visible.

Barbara Kelly, of Huntington, is the owner of the photograph. The youngster proudly standing on the left with his thumbs in his waistcoat is her father, William Henry Radford. He was born in 1896.

Her grandfather, also William Henry, is on the far right. She is unsure who the rest of the party is, although she said: "The lady on the left of the picture sitting down might be my grandmother."

According to a note on the back of the photograph, it dates from 1910. Exactly where the picture was taken is unclear although it is likely to be close to the home of her grandfather and his family.

Mr Radford the elder was a gamekeeper for Sir Charles Wilson, and lived on his estate in Skipwith, near Selby. By the time this photograph was taken it is likely that his son had begun to help with the gamekeeping duties.

"My father, when he was 15, made a fountain in the middle of the farmyard," Mrs Kelly said. "It's still standing. How he had lifted the boulders, we can't understand."

When war broke out, Mrs Kelly's father became the batman, or attendant, to Sir Charles, who was the quartermaster of the 15th Battalion Prince of Wales Regiment. In 1916, Sir Charles wrote a job reference for Mr Radford, who was applying to join the military police.

He wrote: "When very young, he arrested a thief, an old jail-bird, in my orchard.

"On another occasion he chased a poacher two miles and had him arrested."

He got the job.

After the war, Mr Radford became a policeman in Leeds. Ill health cut short that career and he joined his wife Doris in running a corner shop in Osgodby, near Selby, for about four years in the 1930s.

During the Second World War he was in charge of the Royal British Legion Club at Catterick, before moving south to the Vickers aircraft factory at Hungerford. Mrs Kelly was in the Land Army. After the war, she worked at the former Schofields department store in Leeds.

Halcyon days of the marriage bureau....

Rain or shine, indoors or out, nothing, it seemed, could stop the members of York Young Conservatives getting together to enjoy themselves, as this pictures from the 1960s demonstrate.

IT used to be jokingly known as the Marriage Bureau. And the Young Conservatives Association in York and elsewhere certainly brokered a fair few marriages. In its 1960s heyday the organisation provided much more than just a thriving social life, however.

Keith Wood was chairman of the York Young Conservatives for five years in the mid to late Sixties and has fond memories of those days.

The former city councillor, Sheriff and Lord Mayor of York was in charge when the membership topped 200, with weekly meetings often attracting at least half of those.

"It was a time when people did join things, as you can see with that membership," he said.

He jokes that the Young Conservatives' choice of meeting place was "the kiss of death".

Their original venue was the Queen's Hotel in Micklegate – later demolished – and later they met at the Half Moon pub in Blake Street – now a branch of McDonalds.

At each meeting, there would be a political speaker, a general interest speaker and a local speaker. When York University was being established for example, Prof Patrick Nuttgens addressed the Young Conservatives. Another speaker was Josephine Butler, secretary to

Winston Churchill during the war.

Mr Wood said: "This wasn't an out-and-out political association. Yes, it was politically motivated. You did have the opportunity to help the Conservative Party.

"There were many local councillors who were regular visitors. If we knew them, we would go and work for them at election time. People like Malcolm Heppell, another ex-Lord Mayor."

Long serving local councillors John Clout and the late Clive Kay were others to benefit from this team of volunteers.

The YCs would also be out in force at General Election time, canvassing for the then MP, Charles Longbottom.

They played just as hard as they worked. Soon after it opened in 1965, the Cock and Bottle in Skeldergate became their social headquarters. Members of the Young Conservatives also set off for the Lyke Wake Walk across the North York Moors.

Regular dances were held – the favourite group of the YCs was Tony Adams and the Viceroys. Boat trips were popular in the summer.

With all this going on, it is hardly surprising that the Young Conservatives produced a few marriages. Mr Wood met his wife, June, at the meetings, and married her during his tenure as chairman.

Theirs was the first of several weddings among members. The managing director of York-based building giant Shepherd Construction, Paul Shepherd was another who met his wife at the YCs.

Mr Wood, who was a city councillor for 22 years, said: "It was a very good social meeting place and it's true, lots of people did get married.

"In York now, there is a nucleus of members – 12 couples who are still close friends. We try to meet on a fairly regular basis.

"We have still got some very good friends that we made through the Young Conservatives. We have been friends for 25-30 years. Whenever we meet, it's as though there has been no time in between."

In the 1960s, nationwide membership of the Young Conservatives peaked at 500,000 – today it is down to about 5,000. Political and social times have changed.

Gambling fever swept the nation

SIR Stanley Raymond, first chairman of the Gaming Board, was adamant. Badly constructed bingo halls "are dangerous places for such large numbers of housewives to be exposed," he stormed.

Evening Press columnist John Blunt, meanwhile, was more concerned about the hazards inherent in fruit machines. "In Chicago," he reported, "it took the Americans several decades to rid the city of the gangland feuds that began with the one-armed bandits and ended with

The former casino at Clifton Bingo, York

armed thugs splattering the pavements with blood."

Both these statements appeared in the Press in 1968 and vividly demonstrate the gambling backlash at that time. A succession of Church reports condemning the betting industry were published in the late Sixties.

Stories of women frittering away the week's housekeeping and men stealing to fund their habit added to the fears that Britain's moral well-being was in danger. And there were also indications that mobsters were beginning to make inroads into the burgeoning casino culture.

It was this climate of anxiety that led Jim Callaghan, then Home Secretary in Harold Wilson's Labour government, to draw up the 1968 Gaming Act.

This prohibited casinos in county boroughs with a population of less than 125,000. Certain named towns, mainly seaside resorts, were exempt but the act closed all of York's casinos and hundreds of others around the country.

Until then, many people in York had enjoyed regular games of roulette, blackjack and card bingo at four clubs in the city.

Each venue had a different character. The 55 Club, at 55 Micklegate, was for the serious players. Secretary of the club was Neville England, a well-known property owner and restaurateur.

In 1963, two undercover police officers visited the club and discovered "flagrant disregard for the licensing laws in general," as York Chief Constable Carter put it. Fines for breaches of its alcohol licence and for betting irregularities totalled £380.

By the late Sixties it was known as the New 55 Club and was co-owned by Don McCallion, an extrovert Essex-born businessman.

He had previously run the Mecca Rialto in Fishergate, where he presented many pop stars including The Beatles. Mr McCallion later moved to London and became managing director of the chain of EMI Social Centres.

In Bootham, you could find The Society Club, owned by Charles Sykes. This was primarily a restaurant and nightclub and the gaming activities were a sideline. Similarly the casino was a popular extra attraction at both the Mecca and Clifton clubs. Their main draw was bingo.

Frank Allis was in the trade for most of his working life. He worked at the Mecca with Mr McCallion, later moving to the Clifton where he stayed for 20 years.

Originally built as a cinema by legendary York impresario Jack Prendergast, it is still running as Clifton Bingo Club. Jack's grandsons Jonathan and Jeremy later took over the running of the bingo club.

The casino opened in the mid Sixties a year or two after bingo started there, and was run by Jack Prendergast's son Patrick and Jack Senescall. Jack was also an enthusiastic player, and when York's casinos were closed down he would travel to Leeds for a few games.

Clifton's casino was upstairs at the club in a room which doubled as the ballroom. It was deco-

Don McCallion: gambling club owner and entrepreneur.

rated in the best possible taste: the wallpaper was patterned with prints of naked women.

Croupiers would stand in the middle of the purpose-built roulette tables. The tables were made by True View, the same company which manufactured Clifton's cinema screens. Smartly dressed waitresses ferried trays of drinks from the bar to the customers.

Games were played before the bingo started, during the interval between bingo sessions, and afterwards. Jonathan said: "We had a captive audience because we had the bingo audience. It was tremendously successful."

The players were nothing like the super-rich casino patrons as seen in James Bond films. These were ordinary York people, men and women enjoying a flutter – although most participants dressed up for their night out.

"It was a terrific atmosphere," Frank recalled. "That's what made the club, the atmosphere."

It cost 2s 6d in old money (12½p) to play a game of roulette, plus the stake money. Coloured chips were bought at a hatch in the small office to one side of the room.

Bets were rarely large, but even small sums were significant to many of the less well-off participants. Perhaps surprisingly, therefore, displays of bad temper by those on a losing streak were uncommon.

"They laughed it off," Frank said. He added: "We never caught anyone trying to cheat. They would have had a job to cheat."

The casino was licensed to operate until 11pm, although Patrick was often up until the early hours cashing up. He loved the casino. The Gaming Act which forced its closure "broke his heart", according to his widow June.

Club owners in York "played hell" over the legislation, Frank said. They all believed the Act was an over-reaction: "like a sledgehammer to crack a nut", as Mr McCallion of the New 55 Club put it. Overnight the number of casinos nationwide was cut from 1,200 to around 200, and the Gaming Board was introduced to regulate the trade.

Three decades on, the board is set to oversee the relaxation of the law. Casinos will soon be allowed to operate in York again. Clifton Bingo Club will not be able to reopen its casino, however, as the rules state the two forms of gambling have to be kept separate.

But Frank Allis is delighted to hear that the clatter of roulette ball on wheel will be heard in the city once more.

"It's great news. It's very harmless entertainment and it was really good fun."

Getting to grips with a sporting craze

WHEN the noble art of wrestling was at its most popular, it attracted exponents to York from across the globe. Billy Tworivers, for example, was a North American Indian who lived in Canada. He used to arrive in the ring complete with feather head-dress, only to whip it off revealing a Mohican hairstyle underneath.

"He caused a bit of a fashion" recalls wrestling fan Harry Gould. "Kids were going around the streets with a Mohican. They think it is new, but kids were doing it 30 years ago."

Tosh Tojo, famous for his role as Oddjob in the James Bond film Goldfinger, was of Japanese extraction but lived in Honolulu. He was a York wrestling favourite.

Tall and imposing, the west African Massambula strode into the spotlight wearing his distinctive leopard skin costume.

Maori chief Keita Meretana was another regular, and the SS Empire also hosted bouts involving Hungarians, Russians and Poles.

Mr Gould, a retired painter and decorator from York, remembers them all. He became a wrestling fan when he was growing up in Sheffield watching the sportsmen working out in a local gym.

He moved to York in 1949 but had to wait another nine years before professional wrestling was regularly staged in the city. It was put on by Ernest Shepherd at his theatre, the Empire -

now the Grand Opera House.

Mr Gould clearly remembers the first show: Mighty Chan and Roy Foy topped the bill.

"It was a good start. In a matter of two or three months it became a sell-out every time.

"There was a very mixed audience, including directors of local companies, like Taylor's Steelworks of Layerthorpe - you got the screaming women as well. Heavyweights were always the favourites."

Glamorous favourites included Mr TV Jackie Pallo and Jimmy Savile. The bejewelled disc-jockey was a famous grappler long before he used to fix things on telly, although he had already adopted the cigar as his trademark.

Harvey Smith, now better known for his showjumping exploits, was another wrestler on an Empire bill in the past. Pat Roach, who was often in the ring at the Empire, went on to find national fame as Bomber in the TV series Auf Wiedersehen Pet.

Michael Brookes put the fear of God into his opponents: he was a vicar and known as the Wrestling Parson.

In 1968, it cost only 3d for a night at the wrestling. According to Mr Gould, there were two types of bout - the stage-managed fight and the real contest between two sportsmen.

"If you got two good wrestlers together, to me

Billy Tworivers: popular character at York wrestling meets.

that appealed. I liked seeing good wrestling.

"You could also get cowboys and indians - a goodie and a baddie. The crowd starts screaming blue murder."

Mr Gould used to do some coaching of wrestlers in a room at the Empire. One of the favourite competitors from York was John Cox, who later went to work for the North Yorkshire Ambulance Service. Together with Albert Wall from Doncaster he won a championship in Japan.

Tommy Adamson, a stonemason, had to shorten his name to George Adams when he became a professional wrestler. "His name was too long for the bill," Mr Gould explained.

Clubs for amateur wrestlers were also common in the 1960s. Members of one such club practised at the York Rugby Club in Clarence Street.

Some became part-time professionals.

"The trouble with wrestling full time was you couldn't get insurance. If you broke your arm in the gym you were out and you got no pay."

Wrestlers were careful to avoid inflicting real injuries on their opponents - they knew they would meet again quickly giving opportunities for revenge to be inflicted. But there were accidents.

Mr Gould recalls one particular night when Brian Glover, now a distinguished actor, was wrestling on the Empire bill.

"That night two wrestlers were taken to hospital. One was Brian Glover - his cartilage locked with his knee. We had to take him into the ambulance sitting in a chair, At the hospital the doctors straightened up his leg.

"Sandy Orford, he broke his nose the same night."

Eventually wrestling began to lose its popularity. ITV first reduced its coverage and then scrapped it altogether. Youngsters who previously would have gone to a wrestling club were instead learning the martial arts of karate and judo.

The bouts stopped and the Empire closed. But now wrestling is back on TV.

Mr Gould is cool about the modern style, which he believes is too like the American, showbusiness form of wrestling. He hankers after the days when Johnny Allen, Roy Bull Davies, Cowboy Cassidy and their ilk bestrode the ring.

The days when, as he said, "every nationality came to wrestle in York".

York wrestler, later turned ambulanceman, John Cox, in action at the SS Empire.

Celebrating 60 glorious years

STREET parties, mass choruses of the National Anthem, bunting galore. When Queen Victoria celebrated her diamond jubilee, York held one of the biggest parties in its history. There was every reason to make merry. During the record breaking 60-year reign, Britain and her empire had flourished like never before.

Queen Victoria acceded to the throne at the age of 18 in 1837. Her diamond jubilee was celebrat-ed on June 22, 1897.

The city of York had begun planning for the event months in advance.

Following precedent set by previous jubilees, it had been agreed to provide entertainment for the children and the poor.

More than £742 was raised by public subscription for the "day of rejoicing fund". Meanwhile, York Corporation agreed to manage the strays to provide children's playgrounds.

A meeting in the Mansion House in March discussed establishing a suitable and lasting monument to the Queen's record reign.

As a result two jubilee charity funds were set up. One raised £267 for an extension to York County Hospital and the other brought in £738 to assist the York Dispensary to move to better premises.

The night before the jubilee, a special Shrieval Dinner was held at Harker's Hotel in York. Before the great and good started their meal, good news was announced by the Sheriff, Mr Dodsworth.

"I wish to say a word or two that I know you will be pleased to hear," he said.

"I have just seen a telegram from London saying that in the list of honours was included the name of the Lord Mayor to be knighted."

The Lord Mayor, Christopher Annakin Milward, made a speech acknowledging his good fortune in the Queen's jubilee honours.

"The honour is done to the City of York and not to myself. The City of York is held throughout the length and breadth of the land in far greater respect than many of the citizens have any conception.

"A representative of the City of York in any capacity is in a proud position, especially one who represents it as the Lord Mayor."

The Evening Press reacted a little sniffily to the news that the Queen had also allowed other cities to have a Lord Mayor as part of the celebrations.

"York is, and has anciently been, a city, and its chief magistrate has long been a Lord Mayor," the leader stated. "No higher civic honours could be therefore be conferred upon it, as in the case of Leeds, Sheffield, Nottingham and Hull."

On the day itself, the first acknowledgement of the jubilee came with a peal of the Minster bells at 8.30am. As the morning went on, other churches joined in.

It was a dull and overcast at first but by lunchtime the city was bathed in glorious sunshine. Business had been almost entirely suspended for the day and colourful bunting decorated every street.

The Evening Press correspondent was impressed. "A general view of the city at once revealed that a holiday was being kept for, from almost every tower – and York boasts many towers – there floated the Union Jack or some other indication of the loyalty of the city."

Amongst the features the Press picked out as being especially fine were the Yorkshire Club, Lendal Bridge and Coney Street, the latter boasting Royal Standards and banners as well as the Union Jack.

Clifford's Tower was also flying the flag as was

Stonegate, York, decked out to celebrate Queen Victoria's diamond jubilee in 1897.

the Assize Courts. Many fluttered high above Stonegate.

Celebrations took different forms in different parts of the city. At the Infantry Barracks, the Army paraded before Colonel Harington, commanding officer of the 14th Regimental District.

On the stroke of noon, the soldiers fired a "feu de joie", before taking off their headgear and giving three hearty cheers for Her Majesty.

York citizens could gain free admission to Museum Gardens for the day. Many took the opportunity to bask in the park.

A thanksgiving service was held at the Minster. The Lord Mayor led a civic procession from the Mansion House to the great church, watched by cheering crowds.

It was the children of the city who probably enjoyed the day most. Shortly after 1pm, all the youngsters were given a commemorative medal at their respective schools.

Then they assembled at three points. Church of England children gathered at Dean's Park; Roman Catholic children were on the grass in front of the Freemason's Hall, Duncombe Place; and Parliament Street was the location "for the children of the various dissenting sects".

At two o'clock they all marched to Bootham Field, forming a huge crowd around musical director Mr Mills. When he ascended the stand, to lead them in singing God Save The Queen, the children lowered their flags and banners.

The sounding of a bugle was the signal for attention. Five combined bands struck up.

"And then," the Press reported, "at the conductor's signal, 14,000 little throats took up the familiar strains with wonderful unanimity."

After two verses, the children cheered and ran off to try the roundabouts and swings set up for the occasion. Two hours later, they were taken back to school for tea.

That wasn't the largest chorus of the National Anthem, however. At Headingley cricket ground, the Yorkshire v Surrey match was delayed to allow the 30,000 crowd to sing the anthem, followed by a spontaneous rendition of Rule Britannia.

In York, the celebrations went on well into the evening. All the city bars were illuminated, along with the Mansion House, and bonfires were lit at Piccadilly Postern, Lord Mayor's Walk and elsewhere.

But the most impressive display was at York Minster.

"Before the clocks had finished striking the hour of 10 the first coloured fire shed its brilliant light on the sacred building, and the effect was unsurpassingly grand," the newspaper said.

A searchlight also lit up the sky from the lantern tower of the Minster, and the Press commented that it would "be of inestimable advantage in case the city was invaded by a besieging force for its rays would throw into light as bright as day the county for a considerable distance beyond the city walls".

It was the dazzling end of a dazzling day. The following day the city honoured its promise to its poor with a meat tea and games held at York workhouse. Queen Victoria died in 1901.

Keeping it in the family

THE history of Malton's most famous stables, Highfield, is the history of a few families. Hundreds of winners have been produced at the yard since it was established more than two centuries ago. And most of these will have been connected with one or other of the Highfield racing families.

The latest of these, the Hethertons, celebrate the 60th anniversary of their association with the stables in 1998.

It was 1938 when York insurance director John Hetherton brought a racehorse to be trained by Captain Charles Elsey at Highfield. It proved to be the first of more than 200 winners in the Hetherton colours. The family has certainly made its mark on the stables' long and prestigious history.

George Searle was the first recorded trainer at Highfield. His horse Imperartrix won the sixth running of the St Ledger in 1782.

But the first great family name to be associated with the yard was that of Scott in the 19th century.

William Scott was the brother of the "Wizard of the North" John Scott.

John trained a string of classic winners from his Whitewall Stables in Malton, most of which were ridden by brother Bill.

But Chris Hoggard, in his History Of Highfield, revealed how William Scott arrived at Highfield when the brotherly partnership came to an end.

Bill Scott, he writes, was an excessive drinker - along with "a lot of jockeys in this era".

"In the 1846 Derby he had a violent argument with the starter and lost many lengths at the start.

"Having got to the front, he allowed a horse up his inner to beat him by a neck.

"Partly due to this incident the brothers went their separate ways."

When William Scott died at Highfield in 1848, the stables were taken over by another man whose record in racing has stood the test of history - William I'Anson.

He bought what was to become the matriarch of a racing dynasty, Queen Mary. As a two-year-old, Queen Mary won eight races, the most outstanding of which was The Gimcrack at York.

The following year she won both the Derby and the Oaks, a feat only achieved by three other horses.

William I'Anson Jnr took over at Highfield after his father's retirement in 1865. He won the Oaks with Jenny Howlet in 1880.

He leased Highfield to Sir John Thursby in 1908. Sir John built the impressive stable block and clock tower that are still used today. They were constructed to such high standards that they have hardly needed alteration in the following 90 years.

It was in the 1920s when the Elsey family became associated with Highfield Stables. William Elsey had received acclaim for training a string of winners in Lincolnshire.

His son Charles moved to Highfield in 1924. He served as a captain in the Great War before returning to the Malton stables and hitting big time success.

Capt Elsey was the Henry Cecil of his day, training winner after winner. The only classic to elude him was the Derby.

The success of the Hetherton-owned/Elsey-trained horses down the years are kept in a series of scrapbooks now kept by James.

These detail how racing continued during the Second World War - although circumstances forced a few changes in the way the sport was run.

One newspaper cutting, from 1942, records the

Bob, owned by John Hetherton and trained at Norton by Capt Elsey, romps home in the 1951 Ebor Handicap at York.

advancing role of women.

"The shortage of manpower is a big worry to all trainers and like Mr T Hall, whose two daughters ride for him, Capt Elsey also employs a girl, Miss Peterson, whom I saw riding Yorkshire Hussar at morning exercise."

Yorkshire Hussar went on to win the Substitute Ebor Handicap at Pontefract, helping John Hetherton to top the list of winning racehorse owners in the North in 1943.

As well as Yorkshire Hussar, he had several other horses with military-sounding names inspired by the war, including Handsome Territorial, Squadron Leader and Troop Leader. The King had set the trend by calling one of his racehorses Air Raid.

In 1945, Highfield's 14-year-old jockey Derek Stansfield recorded a famous victory at The Lincoln. Derek, who had been an apprentice to Capt Elsey for a year, rode the 33-1 shot Double Harness to a surprise win.

Two years later, John Hetherton and Capt Elsey contrived to make history - by flying horses to a British race meeting for the first time.

Mr Hetherton was on holiday on the south coast and suddenly decided to enter three horses in the Folkestone meeting.

To the great excitement of the press, he arranged for them to be flown down from Yorkshire, accompanied by Capt Elsey, in a Bristol freight plane.

One reporter who witnessed the unloading of the historic cargo at the airfield wrote: "First out of the plane was My Chum, who is engaged in the mile and a half Kent handicap.

"He looked quite fresh after his journey of less than two hours from Driffield, and went off quite

perkily with the head lad and the trainer."

My Chum came second, proving that horses were not upset by the experience of air travel.

Capt Elsey said: "The actual flying was grand. The horses were quite unperturbed, even when the engines were revved up just before take off."

A great victory on home turf was achieved in 1951, when Mr Hetherton's simply named Bob romped home in the Ebor, which, post-war, was back at York.

It was Capt Elsey's third Ebor success and just one of his countless victories that included every English classic save the Derby.

Bill Elsey continued his father's winning traditions for John's son Noel. Their winners included Line Slinger in the Yorkshire Oaks.

Noel, a retired York solicitor, bought Highfield Stables in 1988. Bill continued to train on his 300-acre farm across the road until his retirement last year.

These days, James Hetherton, Noel's son, carries the racing flag for his family. He is not a racehorse owner, but Highfield Stables' trainer.

James trained Past Glories, owned by his father. It became the Welsh Champion Hurdle winner and the longest-priced placed horse ever at the Cheltenham Champion Hurdle, coming in third at 150-1.

James lives with his fiancée Sara and their young daughter in what was Capt Elsey's home for many years. He is proud of the history that precedes him as well as being full of enthusiasm for the future.

"Let's hope that racing will be as good to the Hethertons in the next 60 years as it has been for the last 60," he said.

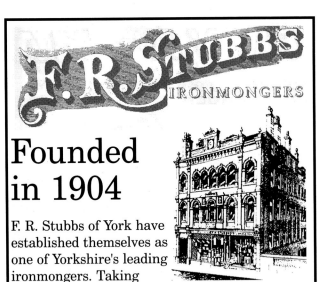

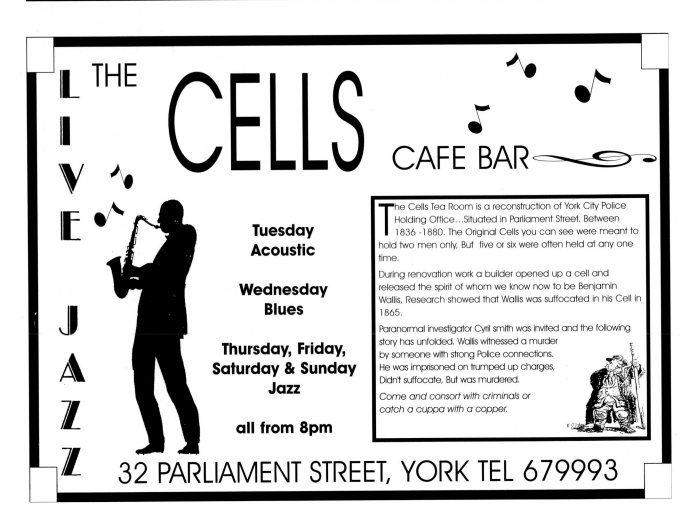

Goodramgate has always been a busy York shopping street but most of the shops in this 1893 picture have long gone, demolished to make way for the opening up of Deangate.

Vital part of our lives

LOVE it or loathe it, shopping is an integral part of all our lives. From out of town retail parks complete with cinemas and restaurants, to so-called sex'n'shopping novels, buying and selling is now marketed as a leisure activity.

How different it was for previous generations.

York's retailing past has been studied in detail by local historian Hugh Murray, whose talk on Yesterday's Shopping In York covered the Roman period onwards.

In Shambles, York is lucky to have one of the finest examples of a medieval shopping street in Europe.

It was once dominated by butchers shops, and was originally called Flesh Shambles to distinguish it from the Fish Shambles elsewhere in the city. Shambles was simply the name for the bench on which the meat was laid out.

Shopping has changed enormously over the years. Once just about everything you needed could be found in the city centre. Now most of the major stores are located out of town in purpose-built shopping centres catering especially for the motorist. Many stores which were landmark names in the city centre have moved on or gone out of business altogether. But some firms have stayed on, adding variety and character to the city centre.

Gone but not forgotten. Leak and Thorpe's (above) was a popular York drapers for decades but the Coney Street store couldn't withstand the financial pressures of the 1980s and closed in 1987. Cussins and Light, at the corner of Goodramgate and Kings Square, was one of York's top electrical goods shops for years. The firm is still in business, but in smaller premises on another site.

Marks & Spencer's York store in 1907 - on the site of the modern Parliament Street building.

At this stage, free market economics had yet to become fashionable.

"Prices were fixed by the Lord Mayor," Mr Murray explained. "He fixed the market prices and the maximum price in shops."

At this time the people of York would shop for the essentials only, food and clothing.

It was not unusual for a householder to prepare a meat pie and then take it to a trader to be cooked. Payment would often have been in kind: for example if the pie contained 12 finches - small birds were a staple of the medieval diet - two would be kept by the cook.

Moving into Georgian times, and the first shops as we know them today developed. Examples of these can be seen in Stonegate. The shop windows are made up of small squares of glass, as glass making technology had not developed enough to produce bigger panes.

These emporiums were for the exclusive enjoyment of the better classes.

"It's not until we get to the nineteenth century that the poor become a significant factor in the economy of York," Mr Murray said.

In the mid-1800s, the Co-operative Movement was established specifically to serve the less well off. The first Co-op shop in Market Street opened on March 16, 1859.

Wholesale prices mentioned from the accounts include tobacco at 3s 7d per pound, sugar at five old pence per pound and flour at 27 shillings for a 20-stone bag.

It was also at this time that York's famous family-run shops were established. Some of the names from the last century live on today, Hunter & Smallpage, Browns, Barnitts and Stubbs among them.

But others have been lost. Evocative names from the city's past include Leake & Thorpe, Lambert's Ironmongers and Aitkins, the surgical instrument makers.

Everything for a penny....

FROM one penny to £16 million. That's the story of Marks & Spencer in York. It opened with the famous slogan 'Don't ask the price, it's a penny'; 90 years on, the store unveiled the multi-million pound store on the same Pavement site.

In the year that Robert Baden-Powell launched the Boys Scouts movement and the Women's Enfranchisement Bill was defeated, 1907, M&S opened its Pavement arcade.

The simplicity of the "original penny bazaars," launched by the shop, meant it was a hit with customers. Shopping was made easy.

Like market trading, everything on sale could be seen and handled. Unlike the market, there was no haggling about the price.

In the shop, there was a variety of goods on sale for one old penny: "a serviceable pepper box, a nutmeg grater, a candlestick, a fish slice or a cake tin" were some of the items on offer.

The shop boasted that there were enough penny toys "to drive children frantic with joy." Men could buy cuff links, collar studs and watchchains as well as brooches for their wives.

It was several years after the arcade opened that the shop front was first installed. It boasted a giant one penny above the reassuring sign 'Admission Free.'

Attractive window displays enticed custom. In one old photograph, an innovative way of attracting shoppers inside can be seen. Posters read: "Come inside and hear the Song Demonstration of all Lawrence Wright's latest song successes. Savoy Orpheans."

The story of Marks & Spencer is a remarkable one. In 1882, a young Russian refugee Michael Marks arrived in England. With a tray around his neck, he started selling haberdashery in villages around Leeds.

Two years later he took a stall in Leeds Market. The slogan 'Don't ask the price – it's a penny' was thought up because he could not read or write English.

In 1894, when Marks had established a chain of stalls in the north east of England, he formed the partnership with Tom Spencer and the famous name was born.

Thirty years later Marks & Spencer had 125 stores and became a public company.

Other landmarks in the business's history include:

● 1928 – the St Michael trademark is first used

● 1975 – shops opened in France and Belgium

● 1991 – sales on the M&S chargecard exceed £1 billion.

During the extension works of 1925 a valuable 17th century carved oak mantelpiece was discovered and returned to its rightful owners, the York Merchant Adventurers, whose crest of arms it bore.

More recently an excavation under the floor of the Curry's building in November 1994 went down into what were once the backyards of medieval dwellings.

Items found included shoe leather, pottery and horn.

Frederick Belmont, founder of the world-famous Bettys Tearooms.

Missed train was York's gain....

TAKE a large tablespoon of Swiss know-how and mix with a generous helping of Yorkshire hospitality. Add the highest standards of service before placing all ingredients into one of York's best locations.

Allow reputation to expand over 60 years and you have a perfect local institution: Bettys Café Tea Rooms.

The St Helen's Square business celebrated its diamond jubilee recently. Now famed all over the world, Bettys owes its Yorkshire location to a mix up at a railway station.

The man who established the business, Frederick Belmont, left his Alpine home for Paris

ABOVE : the bar at Bettys with the famous mirror on which are scatched the names of hundreds of Allied servicemen who visited the bar in the Second World War.

RIGHT: Queuing around the block at the opening day at Bettys in 1937.

at the turn of the century.

He trained there as a confectioner but decided that England was the place to set up on his own.

"I don't think it was quite Yorkshire he had in mind," explained Fiona Hunter, Bettys public relations manager.

"He apparently wanted to head south, to Eastbourne or Bournemouth, where the climate was kinder.

"He arrived in London but he couldn't speak much English. Some helpful chap directed him onto the wrong train.

"Instead of heading south, he arrived several hours later in Yorkshire. Luckily he decided to stay."

Frederick, the son of a baker, worked for the Farrar company, famed for its toffee, before setting up the first Bettys in Harrogate in 1919.

Why this name was chosen is still a mystery. Many explanations have been put forward.

An excellent staff magazine, published to mark the 60th anniversary of the York store, recounts the "sentimental tale of young Betty, a doctor's daughter, who died of tuberculosis and whose father's practice on Cambridge Crescent later became the first Bettys Café".

Another belief is that it was named after Betty Lupton, the "Queen of the Harrogate Wells", and yet another tells of how a young toddler, Betty Rose, burst into the first board meeting while members were considering what to call the new café.

Perhaps the name will never be definitively explained. But the origins of the York branch are more certain.

They can be traced back to 1936, when Mr Belmont, a workaholic, took a rare holiday. By this time he had married a local girl, Claire, and they booked onto the maiden voyage of the magnificent liner the Queen Mary.

"His wife would not have been too pleased," said Fiona. "He spent the whole time making notes."

Mr Belmont was so awestruck by the style and elegance of the ship that he decided to create a new café in the spirit of the Queen Mary. And he knew where he wanted to locate it, as Fiona explained.

"York really appealed to him as a city. When he went home to his family, no-one had really heard of Harrogate but everyone had heard of York.

"I think he wanted to impress his family in one respect. And York was the ideal place for Bettys."

Mr Belmont employed some of London's finest craftsmen to renovate a dilapidated furniture store in St Helen's Square. Suddenly a corner of landlocked York was transformed into the gracious style of an ocean liner.

Exactly one year to the day that Frederick Belmont disembarked from the Queen Mary, Bettys in York opened its doors.

The four storey building boasted the Oak Room downstairs, the café and cake shop on the ground floor, the Belmont Room above it and the top floor ballroom.

The owner's nephew, Victor Wild, who was later to become chairman of the business, was 14 on the opening day - June 1, 1937.

He said: "It was a very grand occasion, everyone in formal dress, the Lord Mayor and civic dignitaries in their gold chains.

"The reception was in the ballroom, and although it was in the middle of the day, the Venetian blinds had been lowered so that we could fully appreciate the crystal chandeliers, the softly lit ceiling domes and the gold satin curtains.

"There was champagne and speeches and applause and lively chatter and the ballroom seemed crowded with bright, elegant people."

In the light of Bettys' subsequent popularity, it is difficult to appreciate how risky a venture it was to open up the York branch. The city had many competing cafés including Terrys just across the square.

But Fiona said that Frederick Belmont's approach to his trade was a key reason for the business's success.

"Now people are very aware of high standards of hygiene and cleanliness.

"Back in 1919 he introduced new standards of catering. He was very, very strict about how Bettys was run."

In 1939, Bettys in York became one of the few cafés in the city to boast a drinks licence. With the outbreak of war and the influx of airmen to the Vale of York, this proved to be one of its greatest assets.

Bettys Bar, affectionately known as the Dive, soon became a popular haunt for the British, American, New Zealand and Canadian airmen. They celebrated to the full, never knowing if that day was to be their last.

The fame of the bar was such that it was even featured in a cartoon in Tatler magazine. When the War Office tried to requisition the bar, resistance was so fierce that it quickly dropped the idea.

There was another nickname given to the Dive. Some airmen called it the Briefing Room – because they could find out all they needed to know about their next mission over a drink at Bettys.

The café's other customers noticed changes, too. Rationing meant that the menu started to offer the unusual delights of fish cakes, spam fritters and corned beef hash.

And one evening an incendiary bomb crashed through Bettys' roof. It was thanks to the vigilance of the café's own firewatcher that the building was saved.

A moving testament to the role Bettys played in the war can still be found on the lower floor. Servicemen got into the habit of scratching their names into one of the many mirrors that decorated its interior, sometimes borrowing a waitress's diamond ring for the purpose.

By the end of the conflict, nearly 600 names had been engraved. One section of the mirror remains on display for today's diners to see.

Sally Carter, manager of Bettys in York, said: "A Canadian lady came in and looked at the mirror.

"Her husband had been based in Yorkshire in the war. It was the first time she had been to England – and there was a picture of her husband on the wall.

"She was overcome."

Six decades after it opened, Bettys is still a family firm. When Victor Wild retired as chairman last year, his son Jonathan took his place.

A large scale refurbishment of the York café has taken place over recent months. The latest stage has seen the Belmont Room on the first floor returned to its 1937 glory and opened for private functions.

All the original wood panelling and art deco lights, concealed for many years when the room was used as joint store and training centre, have been uncovered. An original Spindler marquetry panel has been restored.

And the high standards are the same as ever. York Bettys was awarded the Tea Council Award of Excellence recently.

Frederick Belmont, the accidental Yorkshireman who created this institution, would definitely approve.

Making order out of chaos

CUSTOMERS entering the premises of EH Pickering, bookseller, stationer, printer and general advertising agent, bookbinder, and paper hanger, may not always have known where to find the item they were after.

The arrangement of books and other goods in the High Ousegate shop appeared at first glance to be somewhat haphazard. Volumes were crammed on to shelves and piled high on the floor.

But shop staff knew exact-

RIGHT: Pickering's original shop (on the right of the picture) in High Ousegate, York.

BELOW: Have books will travel. A Pickering book stall at an agricultural show in the early 50s.

An Aladdin's cave of childhood treasures in Pickering's, High Ousegate shop.

ly where everything was, as Derek Reed remembers.

"I was always amazed how the various members of the family and the other assistants could target the thing you wanted and go right to it amongst all that mass of stock," he said.

"I suppose it would have been cluttered by today's standards."

Mr Reed took over Pickerings when Donald Pickering, grandson of EH, retired in 1972. His first memory goes back far further however.

It is of going into the shop as a child at the end of the Second World War. In those days the shop was best known for two specialities, books and toys.

"At that time I would say without exception every boy in York would have gone to Pickerings in High Ousegate.

"It was an Aladdin's cave. It was full of all the great names: Meccano, Hornby, Dinky – that was when Corgi was an upstart.

"Plus there were things for the serious modeller.

"It was before plastic – you would buy strips and blocks of balsa wood to make accessories for your train set.

"I think a lot of the families when they shopped in York would leave children in Pickerings. I got my first Observer book there."

EH Pickering began trading at 28 High Ousegate in 1858. A press advert Mr Reed has kept, dating from the 1880s, demonstrates the bewildering diversity of lines and services on offer.

"Plain & Fancy Stationery," it starts.

"Photograph Albums, Scrap Books, Workboxes, Writing Desks, Tourist Cases, Ladies' Bags, Dressing Cases, Blotters, Jewel Cases, Purses, Velvet and other Frames, Book-slides, and Ink Stands."

That was by no means all. Also on sale were "a splendid assortment of wedding and birthday presents". Engraving, embossing and picture framing were services on offer.

And, of course, the shop sold books.

The Pickering family were committed Methodists. Donald was a member of human rights charity Amnesty International.

"He must have been one of the earliest people involved in it in York," Mr Reed said.

Books were Donald Pickering's passion, and Mr Reed still has the certificate from the 1920s that Mr Pickering was given by the Associated Booksellers of Great Britain and Ireland for passing his bibliography examination.

Another certificate, marking the fact that he had completed their Science of Selling course, was awarded by the Dixon Institute of Scientific Salesmanship.

The family did not restrict their trade to the shop. They would set up stalls at agricultural shows and other events, taking their wares to the people.

The end of a 99-year leases meant Mr Pickering and his family had to move their business from High Ousegate in 1957. After a couple of temporary locations, the shop settled in its present location, Shambles, in about 1960.

Donald Pickering had two daughters, but neither wanted to take over the firm. So when he approached retirement Donald offered the shop to Dick Rollinson, who ran the Barbican Bookshop in Fossgate, and was Mr Reed's business partner.

By coincidence Mr Reed, Mr Rollinson and Mr Pickering are all former Archbishop Holgate School pupils.

Although the Pickerings have departed, the

Robinson's store, South Bank, in 1925. Pictured are Mr Robinson's housekeeper Harriet Killick, her daughter Lily and grand-daughter Elisabeth.

shop has remained a family business. Mr Reed's wife Dorothy and his daughter Janice both help to run it.

They took over in February, 1972.

"Donald Pickering worked alongside us for several months which I think took a lot of doing because we were real rookies," Mr Reed said. "He was very gracious."

He added: "We left the name Pickering. It was his wish as much as anything, but it was a well-known name and had been for a century and more."

They still had no motorised transport. Mr Reed delivered books to schools on a pannier bike, "a la Granville" and later used a pram for the same purpose.

Donald Pickering died in 1983, and a notice was placed in the shop window mourning his passing.

When the corner shop was king....

CAROLE'S Corner Store, which received a number of nominations for our Evening Press Neighbourhood Store of the Year award, is keeping alive a long and important tradition.

Carole Hall, who runs the shop, has won the admiration of her customers for her friendly, individual service.

She delivers goods to elderly people in the area who cannot get out and about, is happy to stock new items on request and always has time for a chat.

That is the same standard of service which customers of the shop enjoyed in the 1920s and beyond, when the supermarket had not been invented and the corner shop was king.

After Carole's Corner Store, in Balmoral Terrace, South Bank, York, was featured in the

York's most famous street, Shambles, pictured at the end of last century when it was still the street of butchers.

Evening Press in 1997, Roy Lord paid it a visit. Mr Lord lived at the shop as a child and loaned two photographs to Carole.

He was the eldest of three children. But his father, like so many millions of others in the 1920s, was unemployed and the family found it virtually impossible to make ends meet.

So Mr Lord moved in with his grandmother Harriet Killick who was the live-in housekeeper for Will Robinson, owner of what is now Carole's Corner Store.

"She called him uncle," Mr Lord said. "My grandmother had been in service for many, many years before becoming a housekeeper there."

W Robinson's shop catered for the population in South Bank, many of whom worked at the nearby Terry's factory or the carriageworks.

It was a typical corner shop, he said.

"You went in and somebody would come and attend to you.

"There was a bell over the door.

"When you opened the door, the bell rang.

"I would often come in through that door and would shout 'It's only me' when the bell rang.

"It opened at eight o'clock in the morning until about six in the evening. On Saturday it would be open until about 8pm."

Although giant, out-of-town superstores were a long way off, competition was still fierce.

"There were quite a number of those shops in that area at that time," he recalled.

The number of traders vying for business is demonstrated by Mr Lord's memories of the fast food trade.

"I can remember five fish and chip shops in that area then. There isn't one there now."

Mr Lord, now in his seventies, was a pupil at Knavesmire School and Nunthorpe Grammar School. He can remember the Knavesmire Hotel being built in Albemarle Road and the shop flooding after torrential rain turned Queen Victoria Street into a stream.

On the picture, you can clearly see the tram stop. He said the trams did a roaring trade on race days.

"While the races were on, there would be trams queuing up from the Knavesmire Hotel to the shop waiting to take the racegoers home."

Mr Lord left York to pursue a career first in the Army for 29 years, then in banking. On retirement, he moved to Stamford Bridge.

When he returned to his former home in South Bank, he was struck by the changes.

The shop has doubled in size, the stairs have been moved and the living space has changed considerably.

There was an old fashioned range where Mrs Killick did all the cooking and this provided the only hot water.

In the small kitchen there was a single gas ring and one cold water tap. Upstairs there were two bedrooms and a lounge which was converted to become a third bedroom.

The initial threat to the corner store culture came with Walter Wilson's first discount store in Albemarle Road, said Mr Lord.

"I suppose the only thing you didn't get was tick, which is what they got from this shop."

But this is one store that has survived all the drastic changes in retailing. Another of its previous incarnations is Arthur Thorn's.

Carole, who has been in retailing since she was 15, ran the shop with her husband in the early 1990s, before she returned last summer to take control on her own.

She said the picture had created a great deal of interest from her older customers, and added: "It's lovely to be part of that tradition.

Little Shambles at the turn of the century: most of this dingy street has now been demolished to make way for Newgate Market.

York's most famous shopping street

TODAY Shambles is York's most famous thoroughfare and a must for tourists. But earlier this century, and for hundreds of years before that, it was just another working street.

Its ancient beauty became evident after modern development left it isolated and exposed. Now it is the subject of stringent preservation orders and is acknowledged as one of Europe's most historic streets.

Shambles certainly dates back to William the Conqueror's day as its existence is recorded in the Domesday Book. The book says that Osbern, son of Boson, received from the Count of Mortain, "14 mansions, two stalls in the Shambles and the Church of St Crux".

St Crux remained at the bottom of the street until 1886; at the other end was Christ Church. As the word "shamble" means a bench for displaying meat for sale, the butchers of York are always likely to have always been a major part of Shambles. St Crux and Christ Church were even known as the butchers' churches.

But it has not always gone under the same name. Once it was known as High Mangergate. In the 14th century, because the fraternity of needle-makers occupied its courts and alleys, it was called Needlergate. By 1430 however the street had become "Flesh Shambles". Of the pubs that used to trade here, The Shoulder of Mutton was said to be the butchers' favourite.

A more cosmopolitan crowd was attracted to The Globe when York was a major port. It was the last pub in the street, closing in 1935.

So it is only in comparatively recent times that Shambles has swapped from being an ordinary working street to one of York's top tourist draws. The publicans and butchers of a bygone age could never have imagined that their premises would one day attract visitors from around the world.

Treading the boards

Music and theatre has always flourished in York, with two major theatres operating for most of this century, and a host of amateur companies scattered around the district. Live music is always popular and York's position on a main rail route ensured that the circus paid regular visits to the city in the past - sometimes with unforeseen consequences....

T HE Redgraves, the Mills, the Attenboroughs – all examples of showbusiness dynasties. But York has its own equivalent family, who have been treading the boards for several generations.

Its latest members to make it in the entertainment world are Malcolm Luker, who now has homes in Munich and Sydney, and his son, Jamie.

Mr Luker, an Emmy Award winner, has carved out a very successful career as a musician and recording engineer for major films and television series and has recently been assisted by Jamie. His movie credits include The Piano, starring Holly Hunter, and he has just completed an Indiana Jones TV series.

In the 1960s, Mr Luker was lead guitarist with The Smoke, who hit the charts in 1967 with the song My Friend Jack. Mr Luker has now got together with former band singer Mike Rowley to record a new album.

Mr Luker's mother, Trudy, lives in a street appropriately named for a showbusiness family – Broadway in York. She has a distinguished history as a singer and pianist, and was known as Biddy O'Connor in her younger years. She accompanied the Irish tenor Danny Malone.

Mrs Luker worked in Singapore, this time as Trudy Connor. She had a regular radio show, even singing in Chinese. The country's department of broadcasting praised her as "an artiste of abundant talent and charm". Later, she performed in her own piano bar in Las Palmas, Gran Canaria.

Her mother, May Passmore, first trod the boards at the age of four, at the Empire, now the Grand Opera House in York. Now in her nineties, she lives with her daughter.

In an interview for the book York Memories of Stage and Screen, she recalled how she was in the Juvenile Troupe, earning 7/6d (37p) a week when she was 17. While on tour she met her husband Jimmy Crasey. She was 21 when they married. At that time, Jimmy was in a comedy trio with his father, James Passmore, and his brother Tommy Hicks. As Crasey, Hicks and Pass, they were well known in variety theatre.

Alice Maydue, a famous singer and member of a York musical family, pictured at the end of the 19th century.

Things changed after the marriage. "Of course later we started a double act," she recalled. "Singing, dancing and comedy. Jimmy Crasey and May Mac we were called.

"May Mac was my mother's own name – her name was May MaCabe but she was always known as May Mac so I took it for my stage name.

She added: "We used to travel by train every Sunday and we all used to meet at the Pro's pub."

In York they would either go to the Castle Hotel – which she ran with her husband years later – or the Lowther Hotel, close to the Empire's stage door. But theatre, like many aspects of life then, was full of divisions.

"We were taught not to mix with stage hands, oh no, we were not allowed to fraternise. That was years ago, of course, it doesn't happen like that today."

May's grandfather Irishman Michael MaCabe teamed up with his brother, Joe, in a comedy act in the 19th century. The Two Macs became very famous, with Sherlock Holmes's author, Arthur Conan Doyle, mentioning their performance in one of his books.

In showbusiness newspaper The Entr'acte, on October 9, 1886, a caricature of the duo appeared along with the words: "If Ireland can send us gentlemen of this stamp, certain is it she deserves to have a Parliament of her own."

Joe Mac's wife, Alice Maydue, was a famous singer and toured the halls to great acclaim. Miss Maydue had the misfortune to be on tour in Germany at the outbreak of the First World War, and she was interned there for the entire hostilities.

The family scrapbook includes another page from The Entr'acte, this time from 1889, with a line drawing of Miss Mayhue.

The news on the back of this cutting puts it into historical context: "Whoever 'Jack The Ripper' may be," a column called Gadfly's Musings records, "he is evidently a man who does things very thoroughly."

To bring the family tree up to date, Malcolm Luker's 22-year-old son is currently studying to be a sound engineer in Sydney, and is a model – the latest branch of showbusiness. From The Two Macs to Ben, this is one family who know how to entertain.

Crasey and Mac: double act Jimmy Crasey and May Passmore, who worked under the stage name of May Mac.

Swing days of the big band sound

TWO former members of the second incarnation of the Modernaires band, Gordon Cottom and Brian Sutcliffe, remember the days when their music commanded audiences of 600 or more.

They recalled how the original Modernaires Dance Orchestra, led by Johnny Sutton, played regularly at the De Grey Rooms in York. Originally a 12-piece, three new musicians had joined in time for its entry into the National Dance Band Championship event in 1950, at the former Rialto Cinema, York - now the Mecca bingo hall in Fishergate.

The competition was sponsored by the Musical Express and featured top saxophonist Johnny Dankworth among the judges and The Modernaires beat off a stiff challenge from the region's major bands to win.

But in 1953, the band split up, Mr Sutton continued to entertain at the De Grey Rooms with a smaller band.

Gordon, a pianist with the original Modernaires, joined with Geoff Towse to become the musical director of a new version. Mr Sutcliffe was recruited as vocalist.

The band remained extremely popular, playing all over the region with a regular spot at the Assembly Rooms in York.

"On a Saturday night in the 1950s to get into the Assembly Rooms people were having to queue at 7.30pm to get a ticket," Gordon said. "At Christmas and New Year you had to get tickets weeks and months in advance. We used to get

600 people every Saturday night".

They performed what became as the classic standards - those Cole Porter, Irving Berlin and Jerome Kern numbers made famous by the likes of Frank Sinatra.

But in the 1960s the golden era for this music was coming to an end. Brian said: "Two of the reasons that big band music fell off were, first of all, beat music came in and secondly the licensing laws changed."

When pub closing time was 10.30pm throughout the week, the appeal of the Assembly Rooms' late licence brought in a lot of people who wanted to continue their night out, he explained.

And the new pop bands, featuring four or five lads, were cheaper than a 16-man band like The Modernaires. Demand for such skilled musicianship dropped off.

So the second Modernaires split up. Both Gordon and Brian went on at separate times to join the Bobby Hirst band.

Gordon also played with the Northern Dance Orchestra and with bands in Scarborough. He is now the resident pianist at Middlethorpe Hall.

Under the stage name Bryan Kenny, Brian formed a quartet and later, a quintet, which also feature his wife June. Today he is a member of the New Earswick Operatic Society.

They still have many happy memories of playing to packed audiences with The Modernaires.

Brian said: "The Modernaires in the 1960s was the best band there's ever been in this town, I believe".

Fans of the big bands mourned the passing of the era and recalled the good times of the 1940s and 50s.

Mrs E A Speed, of Stockton Lane, York, remembers dancing to many of the best known in her birthplace Bridlington. "I've swirled round to the strains of Joe Loss, Harry Roy, Geraldo, The Squadronaires in war time, Victor Sylvester, Edmundo Ros, Cyril Stapelton and Ivy Benson and her all girl band.

"The band leaders all had different personalities - Geraldo was very charming, Victor Sylvester a perfect gentleman, Joe Loss absolutely full of energy. Harry Roy had an 'eye' for the ladies but I always had a soft spot for the Squadronaires."

She also saw Betty Driver "now Betty Turpin of Coronation Street, as a very attractive singer in a sequinned gown."

Harry Elliott, of Marygate, York, recalls a marquee erected in Bootham Park called 'The Big Top' during the war.

"It attracted a lot of big service bands as it was a very popular dance venue," he writes.

"I can remember coming on leave from the RAF during summer 1945 and watching a navy band called The Blue Mariners. The Squadronaires also played there.

"The quality of big band music in York was then first class and it's a pity that 'big top' atmosphere couldn't be revived as the whole place was swinging."

Chaos when the circus came to town....

ELEPHANTS were not an unfamiliar sight in York in the 1920s and 1930s. If a couple of the big, grey fellows walked down Clifford Street today, most passers-by would think their minds were playing tricks on them.

But with regular circuses and animal variety acts visiting York, elephants were regularly paraded through the city centre between the wars.

Several readers contacted The Evening Press after we appealed for information about a picture showing two of the animals in Clifford Street.

By general consensus, the incident took place outside the shop of fruiterer and florist Freddy Nutbrown in the early 1930s.

Mr Nutbrown would not have complained, however. He loved the circus, being a member of the Circus Fans' Association and a subscriber to the showman's periodical the World's Fair.

Grandson Gerald Nutbrown said: "My grandfather was very, very interested in circuses. He knew most of the circus families."

In those days, all the major names came to York: Chipperfield's, Barratt's – whose winter quarters were at Thorpe Underwood – Bertram Mills and Billy Smart. Some came on the circus train, erecting the big top in St George's Field.

Performing animals were brought from the station through York, a procession which did more than any poster campaign to announce that the circus was in town.

When they arrived, Freddy Nutbrown used to supply vegetables to feed the hungry animals.

"Cabbages were one of the things he used to take to them," said Gerald. "I have since been told that you shouldn't feed elephants cabbage before a performance.

"He was circus mad," confirmed Freddy Nutbrown's daughter Ethel Leadhill.

"He used to go and see the performers at St George's Field – he'd go in the caravans."

Apart from the circus, Mr Nutbrown's other great passion was his work. Originally he worked in Charlie Simpson's greengrocers in Spurriergate, winning acclaim for his presentations at the Bootham Park galas.

He was also awarded a trophy for his display at the shop from the South African Deciduous Fruit Association.

When he set up his own Clifford Street business, it was very much a family affair. His wife, also called Ethel, created marvellous flower arrangements. She also cooked up home-made

Two circus elephants enjoy a snack from Freddy Nutbrown's greengrocers in Clifford Street. But the impromptu lunch break for the circus animals might not have been as impromptu as first thought.

marmalades and chutneys for sale in the shop.

And Mrs Leadhill recalls working with her sister Muriel until the early hours of the morning on wedding displays or wreaths.

Mr Nutbrown rarely finished work before 9pm, even taking the trouble to polish the apples so they looked their best the next day.

And he was commissioned to make the official York civic wreath to commemorate the death of King George V.

In 1942, Mr Nutbrown received coverage in the Evening Press for his outstanding Dig For Victory display in the window of the York Electricity Showroom. It included a map of England designed in fruit and vegetables.

Another reader who was in the greengrocery trade, Michael Horseman, remembered Freddy Nutbrown and his love of the circus.

Mr Horseman, who now lives in Strensall, said: "If there was a circus anywhere nearby, he would go to it.

"In the back of his shop he had hundreds of photographs of the circus. It was an archive."

Gwen Townend, of Askham Bryan, said it was not unusual to see the elephants being taken through York.

"This sort of thing was quite a common occurrence. The elephants in particular regularly caused chaos."

Readers also remembered elephants involved in an act on the variety bill at the Empire – now the Grand Opera House – being stabled in the yard of the aptly named Elephant & Castle pub in Skeldergate. The pub was demolished many years ago.

But to discover exactly what was happening in the photograph, we must turn to the account of an anonymous correspondent who witnessed the whole event.

He wrote: "I remember it well. I was about nine or 10 years old.

"Bertram Mills Circus was showing at St George's Field. He had four elephants - the largest was called Birman.

"The elephants were taken on exercise before lunch from St George's Field, via Castle Mills, Piccadilly, Coppergate and Nessgate.

"The barrow in the photo was loaded with cabbages, other vegetables, and fruit.

"It was parked on the roadside outside F Nutbrown's fruit and veg shop, directly opposite the old School of Commerce on the corner of Cumberland Street.

"Plenty of people were waiting around for the 'feed', including an Evening Press photographer.

"When the elephants approached the barrow, it was uptilted and they enjoyed their treat. Afterwards they returned to their tent on the circus site."

So it seems the whole episode was set up as a publicity stunt!

50 years of farces and thrillers....

THE York district is blessed with many amateur drama companies of a remarkably high quality. Across the region hundreds of people are involved in putting on shows from musicals to murder mysteries and thousands more go along to enjoy them.

Haxby Players, one of the best known of the

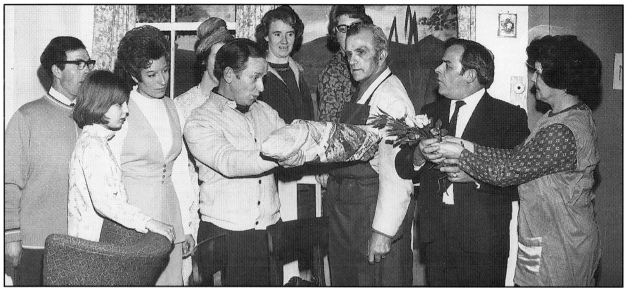

**Haxby Players in the 1960s,
presenting Bonadventure (above)
and The Good Old Days (right).**

amateur companies, have recently celebrated their 50th anniversary. Haxby Players' publicity officer Geraldine Jevons has compiled a brief history of the company. It all began in 1946 when Haxby and Wigginton Women's Institute decided to form a drama group with little success until an application was made to the Evening Institute to enable them to run it as an evening class.

Eventually, the Haxby and Wigginton Evening Institute Drama Group was formed and the class, funded by the old North Riding Education Authority, was taken by the late Miss Doreen Berkinshaw.

Starting with a budget of £20 and footlights made out of old milk tins, productions were first given in the old Wigginton Recreation Hall. The hall was later destroyed by fire.

Classes were held in Ralph Butterfield School and productions transferred to the newly converted Memorial Hall.

It was 1967 when the name Haxby Players was adopted by which time the group was presenting a wide variety of productions not only in Haxby but also in Strensall and Stockton-on-Forest. Passion plays were performed in St Mary's Church and the group scored notable successes in various drama festivals.

Gerald Hansom, joined in 1950. His wife Yvonne's parents Wilf and Rene Barker, were founder members.

Mr Hansom's first production was Time And The Conways by J B Priestley. "I didn't intend being an acting member," he remembered.

"I went down to help behind the scenes, but they were short of men. There was just a small part which I took and that's when it took off."

The Haxby Players put on a spring and autumn production every year, moving into the hall for a week each time. The first few days are spent building the stage and set before dress rehearsals, and that is followed by a four night run, Wednesday to Saturday, in front of audiences.

During the performances the hall clock usually chimes the hour twice.

"It's a bit disconcerting for the members of the cast," said Mr Hansom.

"It starts booming out. But I think it all adds to the character."

Mr Hansom, a retired industrial therapist from Clifton Hospital, who has lived in Haxby since 1939, said: "There's a great team spirit. We used always to have a party on stage on the last night.

"You get to know people. For newcomers to join societies such as our it's a good way to get involved in the community".

He is in no doubt which productions audiences favour most. "The farces go down the best. It's good in the days of television that it's lasted so long."

The swinging section of Selby Toll Bridge which was knocked into the River Ouse in 1930 when a boat called Agility collided with it. While repairs were going on, citizens resorted to a temporary ferry to get across the river. *Pictured supplied by Reg Frost, of Selby.*

Taking its toll of the town

ASK anyone who has ever visited Selby what they remember of the town and the chances are they will say the Abbey or the toll bridge. While Selby Abbey is acclaimed as an architectural jewel, the more humble bridge across the River Ouse has almost certainly had more visitors.

Parliament passed the Selby Bridge Act in 1791, enabling the permanent crossing to be built by driving wooden piles into the river bed, with a deck on top to allow stagecoaches and other traffic to cross in safety.

Until that time, those wanting to cross the Ouse had to rely on boats.

The toll bridge opened for business in 1794, when it cost three shillings (15p) for a coach to cross. It cost a halfpenny for each person on foot, but local people could cross free of charge once a day.

Selby had become an important river port when the bridge was taken over in 1901 by the Percy family, of Hythe.

The structure has taken a few knocks over the years.

In 1930, the swinging section was knocked into the river when a boat, ironically called the

> **Selby, like York, sits on the banks of the River Ouse and owes its prosperity in great part to the influence of the river. It is an important crossing point for both road and rail and until recently had its own shipbuilding industry. And towering above all is its splendid medieval abbey.**

Agility, collided with the bridge.

A ferry service was set up while repairs were carried out.

In 1969, the bridge was closed for major reconstruction. It reopened with a wider deck designed to accommodate increasingly heavy traffic.

But the toll bridge remained a bottleneck on the A19 throughout the 1970s and 1980s, much to the irritation of motorists caught up in queues.

In 1981, the coaster Halscience collided with the bridge, causing some damage.

Seven years later Selby District Council petitioned the Queen for the removal of tolls.

The wishes of local people were finally granted

The Old Toll House, in Selby, pictured in 1930. *Pictured supplied by Reg Frost, of Selby.*

on September 19, 1991, when North Yorkshire County Council bought out the Selby Toll Bridge Company and abolished the charges.

On September 21, 1993, a major mechanical fault was blamed when the bridge because jammed open for about three hours, bringing Selby to standstill.

Last winter, North Yorkshire's engineering manager Peter Welsh admitted the bridge had come under intense loading from juggernauts since the abolition of tolls.

But he did not regard it as being seriously over-stressed and said heavy duty fixings would be used to replace bolted clamps holding together the steel beams and timbers, which were contin-ually working loose.

Local politician Ted Batty called for a weight limit and stated: "No one seems to know what the safe limit is, and they probably won't know until it collapses under this constant battering."

Selby's very own bridge of sighs will remain a major issue until the town's 70-year wait for a by-pass finally ends.

An unusual view of the abbey...

THIS PICTURESQUE view of Selby Abbey (right) provides the starting point for a ramble through part of the town's history. The old postcard of the North Transept, supplied by Selby historian Reg Scott, features a view never seen by people who drive through

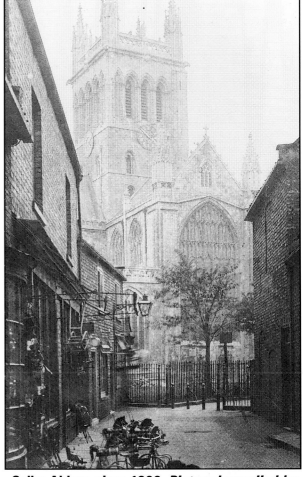

Selby Abbey, circa 1906. *Pictured supplied by Reg Frost, of Selby.*

The swinging section of Selby Toll Bridge which was knocked into the River Ouse in 1930 when the boat Agility collided with it. *Pictured supplied by Reg Frost, of Selby.*

the town on the abbey's opposite side.

This photograph was taken some time after the Selby Abbey fire of October 20, 1906, as the caption refers to the restored tower and transept.

But it cannot have been too much later judging by the quaint tricycles, wheeled horses and other toys spilling out into Church Lane from the shop on the left.

The buildings on that side of the lane have been demolished to make way or modern housing and to provide vehicular access to the abbey grounds.

But the end building on the right is still there, appearing little altered apart from the opening up of a bricked-up window.

It is now used as a Benefits Agency inquiry office. Church Lane runs for only a few yards from the south corner of Church Hill to Church Avenue, site of Selby's cholera burial ground. An old Selebian told the Evening Press that none of the street names was believed to refer to the abbey. Instead, they were inspired by Selby's first parish church at Church Hill. A Selby Civic Society plaque on the railings alongside the abbey states that more than 100 people in and around the town died during the cholera epidemic of 1848-9.

In his book More Old Views of Selby and Neighbouring Villages, Mr Frost says the death toll was 108.

The worst affected streets were Millgate, Micklegate, Finkle Street and Ousegate, all of which are near the burial ground.

Selby's workhouse was also badly hit.

The civic society plaque records that a relief committee visited 800 houses and supplied 358 families with necessities.

It also states the parish graveyard around the abbey was over-used and could not accommodate many of the victims of the cholera epidemic.

This led to land outside the railings being used as an emergency burial ground.

Following the cholera epidemic, work was put in hand to provide a piped water supply and overhaul the decayed drainage system.

Meet the oldest swinger in town

RAIL passengers travelling from Selby to Hull may not realise they have had an encounter with the oldest swinger in town. The swing bridge carrying the line across the River Ouse was built more than a century ago as a replacement for an 1840 cast iron double bascule bridge.

Selby historian Reg Frost explained: "The first bridge opened upwards in the middle rather than swinging as the current one does."

The 1836 Hull-Selby Railway Act stated that river vessels must have priority over railway traffic.

Another old Selebian suggested that the old bascule bridge, which opened in the same way as London's Tower Bridge, may have taken too long to raise and lower by hand.

The replacement swing bridge, which was built at a cost of £22,000, opened on February 1, 1891.

By that time, the East Coast Main Line was also crossing the Ouse at Selby.

London-Edinburgh express trains continued to cross the swing bridge until a multi-million pound diversion took the main line away from Selby and the new coalfield in September 1983.

Only local services now use the swing bridge, which has a fixed span of 110ft and a swing span of 130ft – allowing 60ft of clear water for navigation.

In his 1995 book Railways In East Yorkshire, Volume II, Martin Bairstow revealed that the swing bridge is not a sun lover.

The south side is exposed to more sunshine than the north, causing unequal expansion.

This problem was solved by allowing piped cold water to drip down on to the girders on the south side.

On several occasions in the past, the swing bridge has become stuck or failed to close again completely after being opened to allow ships through.

In 1974, British Rail announced it would replace the water hydraulic system with a modern oil hydraulic mechanism, as well as providing a stand-by diesel electric generator in the event of a mains failure.

Some of the old equipment, by then aged more than 80 years, was offered to the new National Railway Museum at York.

One of Mr Frost's old postcards of the swing bridge features a view taken from the now demolished signal box at the end of Selby station.

To the left of the bridge can be seen the tracks that linked up with the earlier structure.

Another postcard, featuring the swing bridge with Selby Abbey's central tower in the background, was photographed from a point downstream on the Barlby side of the Ouse.

The sailing vessels to the left of the bridge are moored alongside a jetty.

Goods were transferred between freight trains and these vessels, proving that integrated freight transport systems are not a new idea.

Spindly looking pylons were erected on either side of the Ouse to prevent telegraph wires being snagged by the masts of passing vessels.

Similar pylons were known to have been built alongside Cawood bridge, and there may have been another pair next to the toll bridge at Selby.

Thousands gathered to see Hannah die....

THE teenage girl walked unnoticed into York city centre, stood on a cart at Queen's Staith and began to preach. She announced to the world in general that she had lapsed into a trance during which she had walked with God. It was only when she mentioned that a date and time had been set for her death – nine days later – that the crowd began to form.

That young woman was Hannah Beedham, and the year was 1833. Her story is a fascinating insight into the hopes and fears of the poor in York, for they followed her in their thousands believing her to be a prophet.

Hannah Beedham's tale has been uncovered largely thanks to the research of Chris Cade, a

Selby's rail bridge. *Pictured supplied by Reg Frost, of Selby.*

The sleepy village of Kelfield where thousands gathered to watch a teenage girl die.

local history enthusiast who lives in Kelfield, near Selby, where much of the story is centred, and Jeremy Muldowney, of Heworth, York. Together with the Ouse Who Theatre Company of York and the Kelfield community, they turned it into a play.

Their research found that Hannah had been born in Beedham's Court, which was possibly named after her grandfather, in 1813. It was a squalid, disease ridden place off Skeldergate, also known as Hagworm's Nest.

She probably endured an unremarkable pauper's childhood, for nothing is known of young Hannah until she brought her strange message and prediction to the citizens of York when she was 19. Yet in the days after she announced her own demise, word spread - until it seemed half of Yorkshire was talking about it.

The news even reached The Times, which reported: "Amongst other things, she was instructed that her own death will take place on Thursday, the 1st of August; and on Monday next she is to leave York for the house of some gentleman where she will remain until her death.

"Many persons are perfectly convinced of the truth of all the rhapsodies of Miss Beedham."

The gentleman who had offered his house for Hannah's demise was the respected farmer and gardener, James Sturdy. He lived in Kelfield and Hannah travelled there ready for her appointment with her maker which was booked for 9pm on the Thursday.

Thousands of people from as far away as Leeds and Doncaster, made a solemn pilgrimage to be close to this supernatural event. It turned into a boom time for the Cawood ferryman, who did so well transporting people across the Ouse that he made 15 guineas.

As the critical hour drew near, sections of the crowd began singing funeral hymns and many packed into the tiny Wesleyan Chapel in Kelfield to pay their respects.

Nine o'clock came and went – and the news filtered through that Hannah had, in the words of the York Courant report, "remained an inhabitant of the lower sphere". She had not breathed her last, but her credibility as a prophetess had died a death.

The crowds around Kelfield were disappointed, as were the many people holding a vigil on Spurriergate and Castlegate in York who learned of the news that midnight.

The York Courant wrote:

"The hopes of her believers were again revived on Friday afternoon, by a report which circulated through the city that Hannah indeed had given up the ghost, but the fact that she still lived on was again subsequently established to the crushing of those revived hopes."

Hannah was forced to cancel the funeral she had booked at The Holy Trinity, Goodramgate. The fact she had arranged it at all gives an indication of her belief in her own doom.

It was six years later that the funeral finally went ahead, after her death on December 23, 1839. In the meantime she had married and had two daughters. But her 'nine-day wonder', as the press called the Kelfield episode, ensured she was famous enough to warrant an obituary in the York Gazette.

It described Hannah as "the fanatic who prophesied her own death a few years ago and created such a sensation in this city and its vicinity to induce a large number of persons to make a pilgrimage to Kelfield in order to witness its accomplishment.

"Her closing days have been passed in distress and poverty."

How the Evening Press brought news of the terrible winter of 1947.

Winter of our discontent

THE horrendous winter of 1947 began to bite in January when the Evening Press reported that four inches of snow fell over York. This was the start of a two-month period of snow, bitter cold and then floods, which Mrs Vera Seabrooke, from Barley Fields, Shipton, still remembers vividly.

"It was the hardest time of my life. More than three feet of snow fell."

It wasn't just the cold though which created problems.

"Conditions were horrific. We suffered from lack of food, but most of all from lack of coal," recalls Vera.

The coal industry was transferred to the nation on January 1 by Prime Minister Clement Atlee, and from the start, the nationalisation process was hampered by shortages.

The Evening Press's front page headline on January 6 read: "York areas have current supplies cut off," as efforts to cut voltage levels were introduced to save coal used in power stations.

"War rations were still in place, and the coal ration was one sack a week" recalls Raymond Braithwaite, from Cornlands Road, Acomb.

"We had to pick up twigs and we mixed coal dust with cement to make our coal last longer.

"We even put potato peelings on the coal so that it wouldn't burn so quickly".

The Yorkshire resilience was echoed by an Evening Press editorial which read: "The hardy people of York wait for the Ouse to freeze before they grumble."

Raymond remembers how this eventually happened despite the efforts of tugs to break up the ice.

Adversity binds people together. Troubles shared are easier borne and the knowledge that you are not along in your suffering eases the load. Nowadays, with modern communications, disasters from around the world appear on our TV screens within hours. But in earlier times, it was problems nearer home that occupied Evening Press readers. In the Vale of York, flooding was a constant threat, epidemics threatened all and 20th century wars touched the lives of just about everyone.

"I used to work on the buses," recalled Vera. "when I got to the depot, the inspector on duty gave me a shovel and said, 'Here, Vera, dig your bus out.'"

The weather was so bad that bread - which had gone unrationed during the war - was carefully apportioned by emergency food trains which were sent to the most isolated villages and, by February, food containers were being dropped in by parachute from a bomber plane to more outlying areas.

The family home of Frank Handley, of Dringhouses, York, was in the remote countryside of Farndale, north of Kirkbymoorside at that time. And it was a packed house, too – Mr

Handley was one of 14 children! He recalled that his mother Mary was returning from a trip to see the Women's Institute pantomime at Leeds when the bad weather set in.

She got to Kirkbymoorside, and was due to catch a lift with the only form of transport which would take her home – her son's milk cart.

But he said there was no way she would make it because of the snow, so she stayed in Kirkbymoorside overnight.

Although the conditions had worsened the next day she was anxious to get home to her children.

"She walked the nine miles from Kirkbymoorside to Farndale," Mr Handley said.

"The snow was so deep, she could reach up and tie a piece of string to the telegraph wire."

Mr Handley also remembered a story about a neighbour called Mrs Metcalfe who was having a baby that winter.

Miss Addamson, the district nurse, could not get through in her Austin Seven, so a track was dug for her. She was accompanied by the council foreman Bob Strickland to the house, and he saw her safely back after the successful birth.

But the story has an even happier ending. After being thrown together in such adverse circumstances, they fell in love and got married!

Roy Toyne, of Haxby, lived at Loaningdale Farm, Warter, near Pocklington, in the 1947 winter.

"We had no electricity in those days," he said, "and we had no water.

"My father used to go from the farm on the tractor to the village to get water.

"It was so cold. I never went to school for two months.

"I remember my mother doing the washing and hanging it out – and it would freeze on the line."

He remembers the snow being as high as 10ft in places, and the snow plough getting stuck.

A neighbour of his at that time would have been Shirley Kent, who now lives in Seaton Ross, near Pocklington.

She lived in a cottage between Warter and Huggate, and was also 10 years old in January 1947.

Again there was no running water and the family's supplies were brought by horse and cart. But this couldn't get through either.

"Mum used to put bowls of snow in the oven to melt for drinking and washing," she said.

"We ran out of paraffin for the lamp so we used candles – until they ran out, and then we had to sit in the firelight."

The 1947 floods bring York to a standstill - here Rougier Street is blocked by rising floodwaters

Mrs Kent also remembers the mountain rescue team bringing food which was left in their kitchen for the village men to come and take it to Huggate shop. And the local doctor would make his visits on skis.

Engulfed by the waters....

I T was more than 50 years ago, but North Yorkshire residents remember the 1947 flood as if it happened yesterday. After the severest winter in living memory, when the Ouse was frozen so hard that a horse and cart could cross it, came the thaw.

Rivers across the country burst their banks but York – vulnerable to flooding at the best of times – was among the areas hardest hit.

Margaret Firth, née Calpin, of Clifton Moor, was 21 in 1947. She was living in Marygate with her two sisters and her mother when the flooding happened.

She said: "It was colossal, terrible. It was frightening – we couldn't go to sleep because we were watching it go up and up and up.

"As it was going up, we had to lift the furniture up. Anything we couldn't lift, such as the piano, got damaged.

"It's an experience I wouldn't like to live through again.

"The water came over our terrace and three feet into our house. The local pub landlord leant us beer crates to lift our furniture above the water.

And the waters rose: Barker Tower (above) near Lendal Bridge, York, was surrounded by floodwater while the riverside walks (below) between Lendal and Scarborough bridges became riverside swims...

"The house was full of silt and dirt. The RAF brought cylinder dryers into our house to dry it out.

"The lino was coming up with the water. The cooker was ruined.

"We were trying to cook on a little ring, and the bedroom fire.

"The council came out with loud speakers saying we had got to get out."

Mrs Firth remembers a sad story from Marygate. "Where the car park is now there were all houses.

"There was a horse and cart ferrying people out of their bedrooms. The poor horse collapsed and died. It was struggling against the water."

She said there was a flood relief fund which paid for the most urgent needs, such as new bedding.

But it was another, rather special gift that made the greatest impression on the residents – a present from the future monarch, no less.

"Princess Elizabeth heard about the floods. Everyone in the floods got a box with tins of dried fruit and vegetables from her.

"They were part of her gift from the Commonwealth on her engagement.

"There was nothing in the shops, it was a real treat. There was all sorts in it. It was a complete surprise."

Mrs Firth became engaged to husband Herbert shortly after the floods. They married on Boxing Day, 1947.

Terence Linfoot found his canoe came in particularly handy in March 1947.

"I took it to Clifton Ings, where Clifton Bridge is now, and launched it. I couldn't go on the river because it was a raging torrent. I was canoeing around Clifton Ings."

He praised the efforts of the emergency services. "The auxiliary fire service and national fire service, they didn't have the pumping equipment that we have now.

"They did very well under the circumstances, together with the police and the ambulance service."

Conditions in York came as quite a shock to Sid Barnard when he returned from seven years' war service in North Africa and the Middle East.

He had barely been back a week when the deep snow was replaced by the floods.

Mr Barnard, who now lives in Surrey, wrote: "My aunt and her daughter lived in Clayton Street, Marygate, some distance from the river bank. Even so, my eldest brother found that their home was flooded to a depth of two to three feet.

"He took a rowing boat to the house and found they had moved into the upstairs rooms."

They stayed at his brother's house in Bishopthorpe Road until the flood ended. On their return, they were met with a scene of devastation. "The wallpaper was hanging off the walls, carpets, settees and soft chairs were completely ruined and the old iron fireplaces were covered with rust."

Barbara Pettitt was a Fishergate School pupil at the time. She remembers that teachers were determined to ensure her class went on their

Water, water everywhere: Armoury Road, Selby became Armoury River after the Ouse burst its banks.

planned trip to Castle Museum despite the floods.

So they used a York Corporation horse-drawn coal cart. Once again, the water was to prove too much of a strain to the animal.

"It was in the middle of the water when, all of a sudden, it just dropped dead," she said. "We were stranded, right by the Mason's Arms. They got an Army Dukw to rescue us. It was quite an expedition."

Selby was hit just as hard as York. Nearly the whole town was underwater. The only dry area of any note was in the shadow of the Abbey.

The Londesborough Hotel, in the Market Square, was adopted by leading townsfolk as the headquarters of the rescue co-ordination.

Lesley Bond, of Larch Way, Haxby, is too young to remember the floods herself. But she is the custodian of a substantial family archive, which recalls the event in some detail.

Her great aunt, Elsie Small, was the only telephonist in Selby at the time, connecting every call that came through. The telephone exchange was one of the many buildings flooded.

Mrs Bond said: "It was a bit like the war. They all joined in and helped each other."

Her grandmother Hilda Bradley, grandfather, and mother Joan all lived in a house in Armoury Road, Selby.

"They lived upstairs in the bedroom. My granny was very adaptable. They had open coal fires in the bedrooms. It's possible they may have cooked on the fire."

Mrs Bond has kept a commemorative booklet published in April 1947 titled The Tragedy of Flood Stricken Selby and District. It cost one shilling and money raised went to the flood relief fund.

In a foreword the Archbishop of York wrote: "It was only when, from a 'duck', I saw the desolated houses standing in the midst of swirling waters that I realised the extent of the catastrophe which so suddenly brought misery and loss to hundreds of Yorkshire homes...

"The redeeming features to set against this black picture are the courage of the people themselves; the untiring devotion of those who have organised rescue and help; and the splendid work which has been done by both the Army and the Marines."

A printed poem about the floods is in the back of Mrs Bond's booklet. Here are the last two verses:

A Reverend gentleman got stuck in the mud
And cried in a voice, loud as thunder:
"Hi, save me Jack," but we shouted back,
"All right, we shan't want thee till Sunday."

It went on like this for over a week
And at last it began to abate:
The councillors met and are arguing yet
ON HOW MUCH TO SHOVE ON THE RATE.

Living hell of the Somme....

IT was a glorious summers day, July 1, 1916. But it would become a day of living hell for thousands upon thousands of young men. The first day of the Battle of the Somme, said Roger Chapman, of the Green Howards Museum, Richmond, was "one of the worst days of British military history".

An incredible series of mistakes turned a dangerous offensive into a suicidal one. It was the first great Allied attack of the First World War,

British troops go 'over the top' at the Battle Of The Somme, 1916.

1914, and the men of the Yorkshire Territorials march out of Pickering heading for the war.

designed to counter the Germany offensive at Verdun: each side faced one another the length of two football fields apart along an 18-mile battle-front.

But the Germans commanded all the best positions on the undulating limestone by the River Somme in northern France. Generals ordered a five-day bombardment of the enemy, with the intention of breaking through their barbed wire defences and knocking out their machine guns. The bombardment actually lasted seven days. But it failed to knock out the defences or the weapons; the Germans were dug in far deeper than expected.

Soldiers were ready to go over the top at 7.28am. the start of the battle was to be heralded by three mine explosions, but the one directed at Hawthorne Ridge was brought forward to 7.20am.

Mr Chapman said: "No-one seems to know why, except it was being filmed."

If it was brought forward to help the movie makers – possibly the most terrible example of media manipulation in history – it enabled stunning film footage to be recorded but assisted the enemy once again.

They expected the attack was to take place that day; when they heard the Hawthorne Ridge explosion, German troops had 10 minutes to scramble out of the trenches and man their machine gun posts before the Allies emerged.

The Green Howards, officially known as the Yorkshire Regiment, played a key role in the Battle of the Somme. It recruited men from across North Yorkshire and Teesside.

There were 41 Yorkshire battalions including nine from the Green Howards. When the Great War started there was a rush to join up. Boys of 16 falsified their age to enlist.

On July 1, soldiers were told to approach the German lines at walking pace, weighed down with a heavy load of equipment, because the enemy was expected to be in tatters.

That was far from the case. Thousands of young men were mown down in a swarm of bullets.

When the smoke cleared, war was never viewed in the same way again. The Allies had suffered around 60,000 casualties - 19,420 dead.

This horrendous first day was the worst of a battle which was to last 142 days and become the bloodiest in world history. The bare statistics are frightening: nearly 1.3 million casualties, including 420,000 British and Dominion soldiers and 204,000 French troops.

The Green Howards - who emerged as the most decorated of all British infantry units with four Victoria Crosses - sustained 3,500 casualties, nearly half its total fighting strength.

All for an advance of a few miles, which was overturned by the Germans the following year.

Stories of individual heroism are remembered. One of the most remarkable is that of Lieutenant Donny Bell. Born in Harrogate, and educated at Knaresborough Grammar School, he was a fine sportsman and joined Bradford Park Avenue as a professional footballer. By the time of the Somme, he was a 2nd Lt in the 9th Battalion Yorkshire Regiment. During the offensive, he was pinned down by a German machine gun. Using his sprinting abilities and armed with a revolver and grenade, he rushed the enemy position, knocking out the gun. He was awarded the VC. Five days later he was killed attacking another enemy machine gun.

The night the bombers came....

IT had been a quiet night. The brightness of the full moon was enhanced by the wartime blackout below. Then, at 2.36am, York's civil defence headquarters behind the Guildhall were put on full alert by a single codeword: 'Purple'. It signalled the start of one of the darkest episodes in York's long history.

The drone of the German warplane engines confirmed this was no drill. It was too late for the city to have taken any defensive action, even if defences had been available. For a Heinkel 111 plane had already laid incendiary bombs across St Peter's School as markers for the bombing fleet that was following behind.

Four minutes later three bombers attacked across Bootham from the north east, dropping the first of nine massive one ton bombs that were to fall on and around York that night. The air raid had begun.

It was not entirely unexpected. Adolf Hitler was said to have previously announced his intention to destroy all those historic cities marked with three stars in the Baedeker guide book. This was said to be his revenge for our damage to Lubeck, a lightly defended, medieval German city.

Exeter, Bath and Norwich had already suffered from the "Baedeker raids". The Junkers, Dornier and Heinkel aircraft had arrived in the early hours of April 29 to bring the same destruction to York.

Prime targets for the German bombers were the railway station, marshalling yards, waterworks and Clifton airfield.

The station was a major casualty. The 10.15pm King's Cross to Edinburgh express, standing at platform nine, was packed with servicemen. An urgent voice crackled over the station's loudspeakers ordering the passengers to leave the train and take cover.

As soldiers scrambled for safety, the first bomb hit the building. Six coaches of the Edinburgh express were destroyed, as were the lamp room, the parcels office, the booking office and the station master's office.

Fortunately, the signalling system escaped virtually unscathed. Thanks to a tremendous effort, the station was in operation within hours and all running lines were available for use by the evening of the following day.

It was only at first light that the full scale of the devastation became apparent. Of York's 26,800 houses, about 9,500 were damaged or destroyed. Other buildings hit by bombs included the Bar Convent in Nunnery Lane, and Manor, Nunthorpe, Bootham, Queen Anne, Shipton and Poppleton Road Schools.

The beautiful church of St Martin-le-Grand, in Coney Street, was wrecked. Next door, the Evening Press building had also been hit as had the historic Guildhall.

One of the York landmarks to remain undam-

1942 and a city in flames: fire rages along the banks of the River Ouse in York as bombs set alight the Guildhall, St Martin's Church and the Evening Press works.

The aftermath of the 1942 air raid on York: the station (above) and Poppleton Road School (right) are devasted after direct hits. Amazingly, the station was working again hours after the raid.

aged was the Minster. But when the BBC announced this news, the Lord Mayor Edna Crichton reacted angrily.

She sent a telegram to the BBC denouncing its broadcast. Revealing that the Minster was unharmed was, she argued, an open invitation to the Germans to return and "finish the job".

A Ministry of Information officer admitted that an error had been made, not by the BBC, but by an official censor who had allowed the information slip through the net.

The human toll was high. Within the city boundary, 79 people were killed and 238 injured. A further 14 people died and seven were injured in the old Flaxton Rural District, which suffered in the attack on Clifton airfield.

It was one of York's blackest nights. But the many tales of heroism, courage and kindness in the aftermath of the raid meant that the city's spirit emerged from the night of April 29, 1942 stronger than ever.

Fear sweeps the countryside

FEAR swept through Malton and the surrounding countryside in 1932 after a killer disease broke out. At least 20 people died as a result of the typhoid epidemic, with another 250 affected. It was traced to the contamination of the water supply by leaking sewage from the workhouse, where a resident had the disease.

The Yorkshire Gazette, on November 25, 1932,

reported: "All known measures were at once taken and have been continuously maintained to meet the immediate needs of the situation, including the immediate removal from the workhouse and effective isolation of the original infecting patient and of all subsequently notified cases, the sterilisation of the water supply by chlorination, steps for protective inoculation of the public and, of course, the repair of the drain."

Several Evening Press readers have memories of that torrid time.

William Stones was working at Robsons Garage in Malton. He said: "It was a queer going on.

"The country people wouldn't come into town to leave their produce. They would wait outside and people would go to meet them, and they used to wash their money.

"To recuperate from the disease, they used to have to fast for a month. When it was time for them to start eating again, they brought the plates in and they couldn't wait for the spoons and were tipping up their plates.

"People thought it was just a tummy upset at first – they soon realised it wasn't. Every morning you would wake up wondering if you were going to get it."

He said he was involved in installing radios – then a relatively new invention – at places where victims were slowly recuperating, to help keep them entertained during the long recovery process.

Those who died included children, and he knows someone who had lost his sister. "She was a lovely girl."

Another victim was Dr George Parkin, who had led the fight against the disease. "He was a lovely doctor."

Despite the reason for the tragedy, Mr Stones, who now lives at Elm Park Vale, off Stockton Lane, York, said there wasn't great anger about what had happened. "It was one of those things. It was nobody's fault."

Arthur Hall was living in the village of Wharram-le-Street, between Malton and Driffield. He was nine at the time and home was The Red House Farm, now a guest house and tea shop.

Mr Hall's aunt and uncle, Charlie and Lou, lived in the centre of Malton. When the disease struck they sent their daughter Dorothy to stay at the farm, out of harm's way. She was also nine.

But their son Tommy was older, about 12 or 13, so he stayed in the town.

Mr Hall said: "Dorothy went along with me to the village school.

"But the boy, Tommy, he contracted this typhoid. I think he was about the fourth victim."

Tommy died but Dorothy, thanks to her being evacuated to the countryside, survived, and today lives at Malton

Mr Hall, a retired maintenance engineer at Rowntree's remembered the villagers' reaction to the outbreak.

"People would say, 'I'm not going to Malton shopping, I don't want to catch typhoid.'"

William Stones also remembered Dr Parkin, who treated many of the typhoid sufferers, including Tommy, before fatally being struck down by the disease himself at the age of 31.

Under the headline Typhoid Epidemic Over, The Yorkshire Gazette of December 9, 1932, paid tribute to Dr Parkin.

"He had laboured with unceasing activity during the early stages of the epidemic, helping to fight the disease night and day."

Alfred Williamson, of Princes Road, Malton discovered amongst the family archives a cutting from the Daily Express, which also recorded the death of Dr Parkin in Malton Hospital.

"They called him the beloved doctor in Malton," the report said.

"For the past month, ever since it because known he had been struck down by the scourge, the people of Malton have prayed that he might be spared."

The paper also carried a poem by Tracey Archer of Malton. She wrote: "He's no longer with us, he who spent his last remaining strength in noble deeds."

Malton in 1932: a town in the grip of fear.

John William Varley: photographer, amateur archaeologist, entrepreneur, bottle collector and donkey owner!

Recording history

THE marvellous pictures on our cover and overleaf, capturing the people of a byegone York, were, until recently, only available to view as faded negatives on glass plates. They are among a collection of the plates kept safely in their original wooden box brought in by Robert Rouse of Tennant Road, Acomb, York.

Thanks to the expertise of our photographic department we can see them once again. They were taken by Mr Rouse's grandfather John William Varley.

Mr Varley, known as Jack, was a remarkable man. Born in January 1865, he lived in Dove Street with his wife Ada and their family.

They were there in the First World War when a German Zeppelin dropped a bomb which killed

> The pages of this book are filled with the memories of Evening Press readers. The words have been illustrated with a variety of pictures, many of them supplied by readers. The amateur photographer plays a vital part in any local history book, providing valuable pictorial evidence. One such amateur is profiled here: Jack Varley, an amazing man who managed to fit so much into his lifetime in York.

someone in the neighbouring street.

Jack was a lay preacher and a leader at Old Priory Adult School, which was next door to The Punch Bowl pub on Nunnery Lane.

He worked in the railway industry as a draughtsman, designing moulds for the parts used at York carriageworks.

Photography was just one of his hobbies. Mr Rouse said the large group picture on our cover was taken in Hungate Mission in York. The others (right) were taken outside houses in Hungate, an area of York later to be demolished in a slum clearance programme.

Jack Varley also enjoyed drawing. "He was quite artistic," his grandson said. His interest in antiques was richly rewarded when he discovered a hoard of Roman coins in a rabbit hole at Holgate. Mr Rouse is not sure whether they were donated to a York museum. Later in his career, when he was working at the railway headquarters, he took to making butterscotch, selling it to office staff.

When he retired, he took a stall on the market in Parliament Street and sold "Varley's butterscotch at tuppence a block".

Mr Varley also collected bottles – although he lost most of his collection in bizarre fashion.

A friend told Jack that he was sending a present to him by train. When he arrived to collect the gift at the station he discovered it was – a donkey!

Mr Rouse said: "He had to borrow some rope and walk it from York station to Dove Street. They had tremendous difficulty getting it to go up these steps along the passage and into the back yard.

"They tied it to the corner of the stand where they had all these bottles.

"During the night there was an almighty crash – the donkey had pulled over the stand."

The family eventually kept it in stables close by. "One day, the poor old donkey dropped dead. Our family went up the street shouting 'penny to see the dead donkey!'"

Mr Varley was also something of an entertainer. As one of the black and white minstrel group the Bing Boys, he was in shows at the Old Priory Adults School.

"When George Formby's father came to the Empire in York," Mr Rouse recalled, "my grandfather was in one of the backing groups.

"George Formby's father asked him if he would go on the stage with him."

Jack declined. With his photography and other interests he had plenty to keep him busy.

Who are these forgotten people? All we know is that they lived in Hungate, York, at the beginning of the century and their images were preserved on glass negatives by the photographer's grandson.

The Black Swan, Coney Street, York: the headquarters for York Tory party last century and the place where dirty tricks were planned and bribes despatched to lure the voters of York.

Sleaze on a grand scale

S LEAZE allegations were never far away during the last General Election campaign. But if a nineteenth century politician were to be informed of modern MPs' transgressions, he might well comment: "You call *that* sleaze?"

Corruption, bribery, drunkenness and violence were all part and parcel of campaigning in the first few decades of the nineteenth century. And much of it was legal.

In those days, York sent two people to Parliament. It was one of 92 English boroughs where the right to vote belonged to the freemen including, until the 1832 Reform Act, non-resident freemen.

Out of a population of around 17,000, the number of people eligible to vote in 1807 was 2,207. But this was still a more democratic system than the so-called burgage boroughs, where the franchise was linked to property rather than people.

This meant an individual landowner could be responsible for the entire constituency's representation. In Malton, for example, Earl Fitzwilliam chose the town's two MPs.

York was regarded as a plum seat to represent.

"Many of those who stood for York could have remained MPs for other constituencies but chose to gain the extra prestige of representing York,

> **Politicians are all the same, you cry, especially after the longest election campaign in living memory in 1997 left most of us gasping. But was it always the case? Judging by this chapter, today's politicians are angels compared to their 19th century counterparts.**

even if this involved the difficulties of a contest compared with the ease of being nominated by a proprietary borough," wrote Malcolm Ferguson in his political history of the time, York Parliamentary Elections 1807-35.

So the many elections in the early 1800s were always a hard fought affairs. The main two parties at this time were the Tories (in blue) and the Whigs (in orange) and their campaigning generosity meant an election was looked forward to by many York freemen.

Mr Ferguson wrote: "Men representing the candidate, known as deputy landlords, were sent to public houses where the landlord was favourable to entertain customers and give them as much to drink as was considered necessary to secure their vote.

"Enormous quantities of drink must have been consumed in the very large number of public houses York then possessed, and in 1835 George Hudson admitted to publicans' bills of £500."

Perhaps unsurprisingly, drunkenness was rife, particularly on polling day itself. So much so that in 1835, under sheriff GH Seymour laid down the rule that "if a man could stand by himself and speak without prompting he should be permitted to vote".

But plying people with ale was not the most direct way of securing a voter's support. Candidates were not above offering plain, old fashioned cash bribes.

A select committee report on the York City Election Bribery Petition, also published in 1835, found that "it has long been the practice at York that after the Election the members should pay a certain gratuity to their respective supporters in the lower classes of freemen".

One voter revealed that "for the last 60 years he had himself received such a gratuity as often as the occasion arose.

"It appears that in the earlier part of that period every freeman received, on his application after the Election, the sum of half a guinea for each Member, if he had voted for both, or one guinea from the Member for whom he had exclusively voted; but that about the year 1807 these sums were raised to one and two guineas."

Such handouts were often on top of the five shilling daily "wage" candidates paid to poor freemen for their supposed "work" as messengers and runners during the campaign.

As most of the politicians were wealthy men, such cash handouts caused few problems. Tories in particular had plenty of cash: for example, Sir Mark Sykes, MP from 1807-20, was a racehorse owner and bibliophile whose collection of books was sold for £10,000 after his death.

One Tory who bucked the trend was Samuel Adlum Bayntun. He was living proof of the Whig joke that the main qualification to be a Tory candidate was a willingness to spend money - in this case money which he didn't have.

It was usual for candidates to stage parades through York, but Bayntun's was the grandest of the lot. From the Tory campaign headquarters, the Black Swan in Coney Street, a band led a procession of his supporters.

When they crossed Ouse Bridge, guns mounted on boats on the river fired a volley. Then the throng paused at The Mount to await Bayntun.

He arrived to the strains of See The Conquering Hero Comes, and led the march to Micklegate, Walmgate and Bootham bars before returning to the Black Swan.

Bayntun, who was only 25, spent a whacking £8,000 on the campaign. His plan to marry money failed and he was left with large debts owing to coach builder and Tory treasurer Robert Cattle.

Nepotism was rife in York's politics. Whig Lawrence Dundas was York MP twice, and his brother-in-law and two sons succeeded him.

York's aldermen were generally Whig supporters, and were not above pressuring tenants and shopkeepers into voting for Whig candidates.

York Reference Library has a collection of original election posters of campaigns dating back 200 years. Some of them would draw smiles of approval from today's spin doctors.

These are classics of negative campaigning. One, from 1818, draws on York's love of horse racing to advertise "the horses and colours of the riders entered to run for the Parliament Stakes".

This was clearly Tory propaganda. One of the "horses" was a dig at the Whig candidate Lawrence Dundas - "Dun Ass - got by Corruption, out of Aristocracy", while the rider in the blue colours had as his mount "Prime Minister - got by Independence, out of Integrity".

Until the electoral reforms that began in the 1830s, the corruption associated with election campaigns often spilled over into violence. Tory Sir Mark Sykes received a death threat in 1818. In the same year a man taking part in a parade was killed by a blow on the head.

Bribery, violence, corruption, death. It all made the 1997 campaign look like a most dignified affair.

Bibliography

Rich In All But Money: Life in Hungate 1900-1938 by Van Wilson, published by the ARC, York

Humour, Heartache and Hope: Life in Walmgate by Van Wilson, published by the ARC, York

Beyond The Postern Gate: A History of Fishergate and Fulford Road by Van Wilson, published by the ARC, York

Looking Back At Layerthorpe: A York Suburb by Avril Webster, published by QED Books

Photographs and Photographers of York: The Early Years 1844-79 by Hugh Murray, published by YASAS

Askham Bryan Remembered II by Mary Carbert

Willingly To School by Margaret Mann Phillips

A History of the York-Scarborough Railway by Bill Fawcett, published by Hutton Press

Blue Coat: Grey Coat – The Blue & Grey Coat Schools and St Stephen's Home of York 1705-1983 by WB Taylor, published by Sessions of York

York Then & Now and York Then & Now 2 by Ron Godfrey and Martin Lacy, published by The Evening Press, York

York Memories Of Stage And Screen by York Oral History Project